PANZERARTILLERIE

OSPREY
PUBLISHING

PANZERARTILLERIE

Thomas Anderson

OSPREY PUBLISHING
Bloomsbury Publishing Plc
PO Box 883, Oxford, OX1 9PL, UK
1385 Broadway, 5th Floor, New York, NY 10018, USA
E-mail: info@ospreypublishing.com
www.ospreypublishing.com

OSPREY is a trademark of Osprey Publishing Ltd

First published in Great Britain in 2019

ISBN: HB 978 1 4728 2024 2
eBook 978 1 4728 2026 6
ePDF 978 1 4728 2025 9
XML 978 1 4728 2673 2

19 20 21 22 23   10 9 8 7 6 5 4 3 2 1

Conceived and edited by Jasper Spencer-Smith
Design by Briony Hartley
Index by Shaun Barrington
Produced by Editworks Limited, Bournemouth BH1 4RT, UK
Originated by PDQ Digital Media Solutions, Bungay, UK
Printed in China through World Print Ltd.

Osprey Publishing supports the Woodland Trust,
the UK's leading woodland conservation charity.

To find out more about our authors and books visit
www.ospreypublishing.com. Here you will find extracts,
author interviews, details of forthcoming events and
the option to sign up for our newsletter.

FSC
www.fsc.org
MIX
Paper from
responsible sources
FSC® C014688

CONTENTS

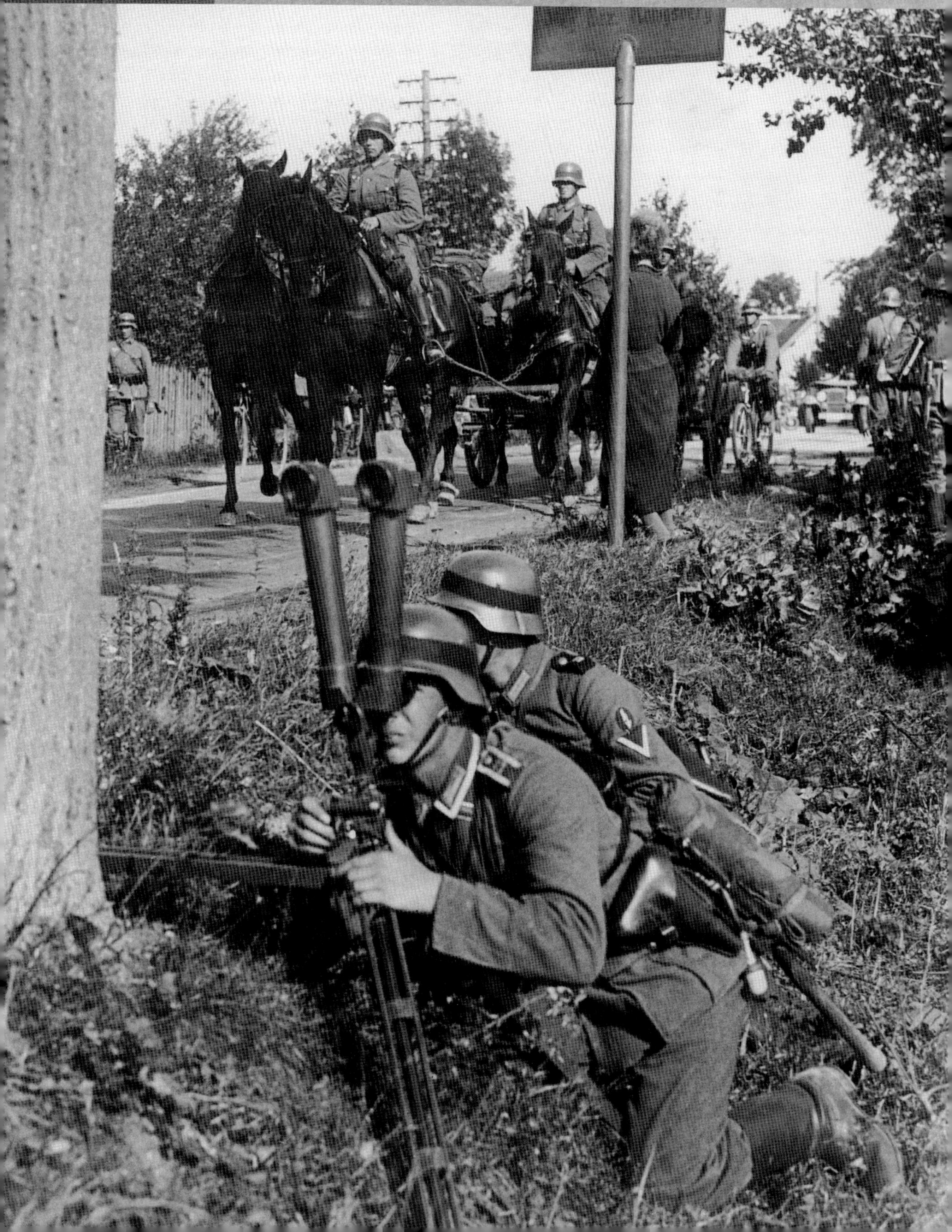

INTRODUCTION

In 1931, *Oberstleutnant* Heinz Guderian joined the staff of General Oswald Lutz at the *Inspektion der Krafttruppen* (inspectorate of mechanized troops) and it soon became apparent that both were in agreement that plans needed to be laid for a revolutionary highly mobile tank corps – the *Panzerwaffe*. The main element would be the Panzer division; a large unit that was to be motorized and equipped with the latest tanks and transport vehicles. In combat, the tanks would strike at a selected point in enemy lines, make the breakthrough then fan out to destroy enemy forces and other tactical targets in rear positions.

Mobile Artillery

Both Lutz and Guderian were fully aware that these rapidly advancing forces would require artillery support weapons which were able to equal the mobility and speed of the tanks. For military planners, totally aware of the lack of support artillery for the Panzer divisions, the only solution was to order the development of armoured self-propelled guns: Germany was most certainly technically capable, but there would always be a decisive gap between development skills and a lack of production capacity, exacerbated by a severe lack of funding.

By 1936, the first half-tracked self-propelled gun had been designed by Rheinmetall. It was armed with a 3.7cm FlaK 43/1 L/70 gun, mounted in a small open turret, and built using the chassis of a Hansa-Loyd HLkl 3. A short time later, Büssing-NAG produced a similar type of vehicle on their BNL6 chassis, but it was more heavily armed with a 7.5cm L/40.8 gun. Both types were intended to operate in the tank destroyer role; the Bussing-Nag type would have been a formidable light field gun to provide supporting fire. Finally, Hanomag developed a reconnaissance vehicle based on their H 8(H) chassis. None of the three types progressed beyond the prototype stage.

A photograph taken for propaganda purposes in East Prussia at the beginning of *Unternehmen* (Operation) Barbarossa of a *vorgeschobener-Beobachter* (forward observer) team positioned in a ditch. The *Scherenfernrohr* (scissors-type telescope) has been mounted on a tripod which has been lowered to its minimum position, but the team does not have a field telephone or radio to contact their battery.

As war approached, military planners selected two heavy artillery pieces – *schwere* (s – heavy) 10cm *Kanone* (K – cannon) 18 and the 12.8cm *Flugabwehrkanone* (FlaK – anti-aircraft gun) – to be mounted on a fully tracked chassis. A small number of both types was built, but were only used for very specific combat missions.

In 1940, it was decided to mount a 15cm sIG 33, heavy infantry gun, on the chassis of a PzKpfw I, now considered obsolete on the battlefield. Designated 15cm *schwere* (s – heavy) *Infanteriegeschütz* (IG – infantry gun) 33 *auf Fahrgestell* (on the chassis) of a *Panzerkampfwagen* (PzKpfw – tank) I, *Ausführung* (Ausf – model) B, it must be considered to be the first German self-propelled artillery gun to be used in action.

Up until 1943, the Reich had not able to build new facilities or increase production capacity for urgently required new weapons. Indeed, the first self-propelled artillery gun manufactured in substantial numbers for German forces would be built using the chassis of a French-built *Beutepanzer* (captured tank). In 1943, the *Wehrmacht* finally took delivery of self-propelled heavy artillery guns mounting a 10.5cm leFh 18 or 15cm sFH 18, and these soon formed the backbone of the divisional artillery. At the same time a new branch of the military was born: the *Panzerartillerie*.

During research for this book a large amount of documentation was found including development orders for a number of self-propelled guns and the directives issued for the establishment of units and tactical requirements. Also the documentation included a number of after-action reports which detail the experiences of troops on the frontline.

A *Wespe* battery of SS-PzArtRgt 5 Wiking on the march in the winter of 1943: The *Panzerbefehlswagen* (PzBefWg - command tank) III is from the regimental staff section, which in turn reports to the divisional staff. The PzBefWg has been fitted with extra armour and a full set of *Panzerschürzen* (side skirts).

Above: *Hummel* self-propelled guns from 9.SS-PzDiv Hohenstaufen being loaded onto railway wagons ready to be transported to Budapest. At the beginning of 1945, the unit was part of the force sent in an attempt to relieve the Hungarian capital from the Red Army.

Left: Thoroughly whitewashed to blend in with the snow-covered terrain, a *Wespe* from 2.SS-PzDiv Das Reich moves to forward in support of the advancing tank force. The water-soluble paint washed off easily which required it to be frequently refreshed by the crew.

A 15cm sFH 18 heavy field howitzer firing at night: The explosive effect of the shell on the target could cause massive destruction and also panic among enemy troops. But the muzzle flash could reveal the position of the battery, resulting in a counter bombardment.

1

GERMAN ARTILLERY IN 1933

The Industrial Revolution, which began in 1790 and continued for some 80 years, was a period of invention, innovation and technical advancement when a number of specialized machine tools were developed; many of which were eagerly adopted by armaments manufacturers to produce more powerful weapons. Their factories, where machinery had been driven by the power of the waterwheel, changed over to the more efficient stationary steam engine.

By the 1850s, almost the whole of Europe was becoming criss-crossed by an ever-growing network of railways; a resource that was soon recognized by military planners as a means by which to rapidly transport large contingents of troops, their equipment, heavy weapons and also supplies to distant battlefronts.

The development of the machine gun significantly increased the firepower of the infantry; during the trench-to-trench fighting of World War I, a single machine-gun position could subdue an infantry assault. This and the constant artillery bombardment led to many years of stalemate.

The tank was originally designed as a breakthrough vehicle to overrun an entrenched enemy and allow the following infantry to establish a new frontline. That was the theory; however, the first tanks were unreliable and often failed on the battlefield leaving the infantry isolated; it would be some 20 years before the true potential of the type would be realized.

In 1855, the British armaments manufacturer Elswick Ordnance Company produced the first rifle-bore cannon to a design by Sir W. G. Armstrong – the rifling forced the shell to spin on its horizontal axis after firing, thus improving accuracy.

In March 1898, the French army took delivery of the revolutionary *Canon de 75 modèle 1897* (frequently referred to as the first 'modern' field gun) which was equipped with a hydro-pneumatic recoil system. The recoil system allowed

The 15cm sFH 18 was the mainstay of the German divisional artillery. Gun 'D' (Dora) is being prepared for action in the cover of woodland by the crew. The wheels are fitted with solid rubber tyres indicating that this gun would be towed by a motor vehicle, usually an s ZgKw 8 t (SdKfz 7).

The *Canon de 75 modèle* 1897 revolutionized the design of a field gun. It was fitted with a recoil mechanism that would copied by armament manufacturers around the world. The gun would remain in active service with a number of armies for decades.

a significant increase in the rate of fire since the gun did not move out of position after firing; also the reduction in recoil forces increased the service life of the gun carriage. A further benefit of a stable firing platform was that it made the weapon suitable to be used as an anti-aircraft (AA) gun.

At the outbreak of World War I (29 July 1914) many of the artillery pieces then in service on both sides had a rifle-bore barrel and were fitted with some form of recoil mechanism.

As the war progressed, it developed into a stalemate where the opposing forces faced each other from established trench systems, separated by a no-man's land of flooded shell craters and barbed wire, where they would be subjected to sporadic fire from artillery; any movement out of a trench would be met by machine-gun fire. An attack by infantry to gain ground – on many occasions just a few metres – would usually be lost in a counterattack preceded by several hours of artillery bombardment. However, despite both sides deploying an increasing number of artillery pieces (including heavy mortars), the infantry war drew to an inevitable stalemate.

An article published in the January 1944 issue of *Wehrtechnische Monatshefte* (ordnance report) provides some interesting statistics. In earlier campaigns fought by German forces throughout the 1800s, the ratio of guns and mortars issued to the field army increased from to 2 to 4.5 pieces per 1,000 men, and in August 1914 this number had been reduced to 3.2, but by March 1918 it reached a peak of 5.8.

However, it was standard practice to mass artillery at a point of main effort or in preparation for an important offensive; for the Battle of Sedan (1870) 4.5 guns per 1,000 men were deployed; for the attack on Verdun in 1916 this number was increased to 15.9, and for the assault of Chemin de Dames Ridge, during the Third Battle of Aisne (May/June 1918), the ratio had increased to 40 guns. It must be remembered that over the course of the war the strength of the German army had increased from 2,100,000 (1914) to 4,500,000 men (1918).

Average ammunition consumption per gun had also increased considerably. During the Franco-Prussian War (Franco-German War; 19 July 1870 – 28 January 1871) each gun deployed by the German artillery fired 35 rounds per month. In 1918, the final year of World War I, this had increased to 704 rounds.

At the outbreak of war in 1914, German artillery had 6,800 light and heavy artillery pieces, but by the end of the war this number had been increased to 17,300 – in the same period the French army had 4,200 guns in service which increased to 10,800 by 1918. It can be assumed that the British Expeditionary Force deployed similar numbers, but by the end of the war they held a decisive superiority when bolstered by the guns of their allies.

Versailles — a Catastrophe for Germany

After the end of World War I, the German Reich was held solely responsible for the conflict. The Treaty of Versailles – 75,000 words, 440 clauses, 200 pages – was signed on 28 June 1919 and detailed reparations to be made by Germany. These included the assignment of large areas of the German Empire, severe restrictions on the production of weapons and also the formation of military forces.

For the victorious allies their aim was to prevent the Reich from building an offensive military capability in the future: German forces would never be capable of fighting another war as the *Reichsheer* (army) would be restricted to 100,000 men. The ban also included the production of tanks, aircraft and other sophisticated military equipment and a strict limitation was placed on the number of infantry and artillery weapons.

Artillery of the *Reichsheer*

The artillery formations of the 100,000-man army were equipped with guns and ancillary equipment left over from the war, but due to the lack of any military planning these were issued to units in an arbitrary manner.

A German document dated 1922 details the amount and type of equipment allowed for the army and the artillery.

Reichsheer (German field army) Artillery
Limitations set by the Treaty of Versailles

WEAPON	7.7cm FK 16	7.7cm FK 96/16	7.7cm FK on truck	10.5cm FH 16	15cm FH	10cm K 17	15cm K 16	21cm Mörser
Field units	140	28	28	84	0	0	0	0
Replacements	2	1	0	2	0	0	0	0
Training facilities	19	5	0	18	2	2	1	1
Totals	161	34	28	104	2	2	1	1

Artillery in Fortresses
Limitations set by the Treaty of Versailles

WEAPON	7.7cm FK16 or 7.7cm IG 18	10.5cm leFH 16	10.5cm FlaK	8.8cm FlaK	7.62cm FlaK	10cm K 17	15cm K 17	15cm K (Kasten-lafette)	lange 15cm sFH 13	lange 21cm Mörser	28cm K (kasten-lafette)	21cm K
Pillau and Swinemünde	0	0	6	6	2	8	18	4	120	14	4	6
Königsberg, Küstrin, Lötzen	92	26	20	20	14	198	60	0	0	28	0	0
Total	92	26	26	26	16	206	78	4	120	42	4	6

Light Field Guns and Howitzers

During World War I, the majority of light divisional artillery units were issued with the 7.7cm *Feldkanone* (FK – field gun) 96/16 and the later FK 16 – over 3,000 of which were manufactured and supplied to the military.

In the early 1930s, the more numerous FK 96/16 was chosen for modification, as part of an artillery standardization programme, to fire 7.5cm ammunition and was re-designated *Feldkanone 16 neue Art* (nA – new version).

Above: Although the 7.5cm FK 16 *neue Art* (nA – new version) first entered service in World War I, many served with a number of German units in World War II. The gun was placed on a small rubber-wheeled trolley to allow it to be towed, in this instance by a British-built Universal Carrier captured during the invasion of France.

Left: The 7.5cm FK 16 nA was of conventional design, but was certainly influenced by the French-built *Canon de* 75 *modèle* 1897.

The 10.5cm leFH 16 first entered service with the *Reichwehr* and remained in use after the formation of the *Wehrmacht* and into World War II. A special single-axle trailer allowed the gun to be towed by a vehicle, here a Henschel 33 D1.

7.5cm FK 16 nA

Calibre	7.5cm
Weight (travelling)	2,800kg
Weight (ready to fire)	1,524kg
Range (maximum)	12,875m
Range (effective)	2,000 to 10,000m
Rate of fire (maximum)	8rpm
Muzzle velocity	660mps
Able to fire gas/smoke	Yes
Transport	Six horses or vehicle towed

When the gun first entered service it was standard practice for it to be hauled by a team of six horses, but when in service with the *Reichswehr* (later *Wehrmacht*) it was often mounted on a *Räderlafette* (single-axle carriage) and towed by a motor vehicle.

A small number of 10.5cm leFH 16 had also been delivered to the military. Although the shell it fired was slightly smaller, the 7.7cm was filled with an improved charge which gave more destructive power. Also the gun could fire at a higher trajectory to effectively attack dug-in positions, trenches and buildings. On many occasions, *Reichswehr* engineers would fabricate a trailer from whatever material was to hand. The leFH 16 remained the main ordnance of the divisional artillery until the 10.5cm leFH 18 entered service.

10.5cm leFH 16	
Calibre	10.5cm
Weight (travelling) position	N/A
Weight (ready to fire)	1,525kg
Range (maximum)	9,125m
Range (effective)	1,000 to 8,000m
Rate of fire (maximum)	5rpm (max)
Muzzle velocity	395mps
Able to fire gas/smoke	Yes
Transport	six horses or vehicle towed

Medium and Heavy Field Guns

During World War I, large numbers of low-trajectory medium and heavy field guns were positioned along the battlefront to provide long-range artillery support.

In 1917, the 10cm *Kanone* (K – cannon) 17 was a straightforward development of the earlier 10cm K 14 to increase performance and although designated as a 10cm, the bore was actually 10.5cm. Long-range artillery was considered essential to allow soft targets, transport infrastructure and supply echelons to be attacked. To improve the range of the K 14, the calibre length of the gun barrel was increased to produce a higher muzzle velocity. When compared to the K 14, the K 17 was much heavier and had to be split into two loads to facilitate transport: as with other artillery pieces of the period, the gun was mounted on a box-trail carriage. During the 1930s, the design of the gun was simplified so that it could be towed by a motor vehicle (half-track tractor) and re-designated 10cm K 17/04.

Two 10cm K 17 in open positions during military manoeuvres in the early 1930s: Unlike all later German heavy artillery pieces, the gun is fitted with a gun shield to protect the crew against small arms fire and shrapnel.

10cm Kanone 17 & 17/04

Calibre	10.5cm
Weight (travelling)	2,837kg*
Weight (ready to fire)	3,272kg*
Range (maximum)	16,500m
Range (effective)	4,000 to 14,000m
Rate of fire (maximum)	4rpm
Muzzle velocity	698mps
Able to fire gas/smoke	No
Transport	12 horses (K 17) or vehicle towed (K 17/04)

* Data varies according to source

In 1917, the 15cm K 16 also entered service with independent *Heeresartillerie* (army artillery) units and was deployed, like the 10cm K 17, against long-range targets. In World War I service, the gun was divided into two loads, each hauled by a team of eight or ten horses, for transportation to a new position. Photographs taken in the late 1930s, and later in World War II, show the K 16 being towed by two SdKfz 7 *mittlere Zugkraftwagen* (m ZgKw – medium half-track tractor) or two SdKfz 8 *schwere Zugkraftwagen* (s ZgKw – heavy half-track tractor).

15cm Kanone 16

Calibre	15cm
Weight carriage (travelling)	6,320kg
Weight barrel (travelling)	8,300kg
Weight (ready to fire)	10,870kg
Range (maximum)	22,500m
Range (effective)	5,000 to 20,000m
Rate of fire	1 to 1.5rpm
Muzzle velocity	757mps
Able to fire gas/smoke	No
Transport	Two horse teams or vehicle towed

The 15cm K 16, heavy field gun could be used for flat trajectory fire similar to the K 17. The box trail-type carriage was a hindrance to the gun crew, as the barrel had to be lowered after every shot to clear the breech and reload.

Heavy Field Howitzers

The *lange* (long) 15cm *schwere Feldhaubitze* (sFH – heavy field howitzer) 13 entered service in the early months of 1917. The gun was a modified version of the earlier 15cm *Haubitze* (H – howitzer) L/14, with the gun barrel being replaced by a new longer L/17 barrel. The range increased by 15 percent making the gun ideal for attacking soft targets and a pin-point target such as a dug-in artillery position, field fortifications and barbed-wire obstacles.

Above: The 15cm sFH 13 L/17 was fitted with a longer barrel which gave an increase of 1,500m in maximum range over the earlier 15cm sFH 13 L/14.

Right: The 15cm sFH 13 weighed some 2,540kg and was placed on a special four-wheeled trailer to facilitate it being towed by a motor vehicle: here an early production SdKfz 7.

15cm sFH 13 (*lange*)

Calibre	15cm
Weight (travelling)	3,030kg
Weight (ready to fire)	2,250kg
Range (maximum)	8,500m
Range (effective)	2,000 to 8,000m
Rate of fire (maximum)	4rpm
Muzzle velocity	381mps
Able to fire gas/smoke	Yes
Transport	Six horses or vehicle towed

The Inter-war Period

Despite the restrictions imposed on Germany in The Treaty of Versailles, the development of new weapons (much of which was carried out in strict secrecy) continued apace. Two companies, established armaments manufacturers Rheinmetall and Krupp, were contracted to design and produce a range of weapons in the following categories:

Infantry guns	– 7.5 and 15cm
Light field artillery	– 10.5cm
Heavy field artillery	– 15, 17 and 21cm
Special artillery	– various weapons

Infantry Guns

During World War I, Germany introduced large numbers of trench mortars for the front-line infantry. These high-trajectory weapons were used to great effect against entrenched enemy troops, but after the war this somewhat crude and bulky weapon would be superseded by the system Brand mortar.

France introduced a 37mm field gun into service which, unlike the mortar, was deployed to attack a specific infantry target. Germany followed and began work on the development of a light infantry gun.

In late 1920, Krupp completed work on a 7.7cm *Infanteriegeschütz* (IG – infantry gun) 18 Kp (Kp – Krupp) which, although the weapon did not see action during the war, was supplied to German forces in the 1920s.

Apparently the German military recognized the tactical advantage of small calibre artillery for the infantry. In late 1920s, Rheinmetall began the development of a gun capable of firing the new standard 7.5cm ammunition. Initially the gun was designated the 7.5cm *leichter Minenwerfer* 18 (light mine thrower)

In 1933, the 7.5cm leIG 18, originally designated a *leichter Minenwerfer* (le MW – light mine thrower) began to be fitted with rubber tyres to allow the gun to be towed by a motor vehicle. The gun is painted in *Reichswehr*-pattern three-tone camouflage.

as part of a large-scale policy to conceal development of new weapons. Later the designation *7.5cm leichtes Infanteriegeschütz* (leIG – light infantry gun) 18 would be used.

7.5cm leIG 18	
Calibre	7.5cm
Weight (travelling)	516kg vehicle 400kg horse drawn
Weight (ready to fire)	510kg vehicle 400kg horse drawn
Range (maximum)	4,600m
Rate of fire (maximum)	8 to 12rpm
Muzzle velocity	260mps
Able to fire gas/smoke	No
Transport	Horse or vehicle towed

In 1927, Rheinmetall began the development of a heavy infantry gun, but for an unknown reason the work on this new weapon was not cloaked in secrecy. The gun was designated 15cm *schwere Infanteriegeschütz* (sIG – heavy infantry gun) 33, and like the 7.5cm leIG, it was able to fire at high trajectories to attack enemy troops positioned field fortifications.

15cm sIG 33

Calibre	15cm
Weight (travelling)	1,825kg vehicle 1,770kg horse drawn
Weight (ready to fire)	1,800kg vehicle 1,750kg horse drawn
Range (maximum)	4,780m
Rate of fire (maximum)	3 to 4rpm
Muzzle velocity	240mps
Able to fire gas/smoke	N/A
Transport	Horse or vehicle towed

The le MW 18 was attached to a standard type of gun limber designed for 7.5cm field guns and pulled by two horses, to carry the crew and ammunition. On the battlefront the gun would pulled by two of the crew wearing special harnesses.

The 10.5cm leFH 18 and limber was normally towed by a team of six horses. The gun is in service with a *Gebirgsdivision* (GebDiv – mountain division); the terrain suggests it was photographed during the Balkan campaign.

A Field Howitzer for the Divisional Artillery

During World War I, German divisional artillery was mainly issued with 7.7cm artillery, but a far-reaching decision was taken as the new weapons were under development. Instead of making simple modifications to upgrade the 7.7cm guns, it was decided to introduce a 10.5cm light field howitzer into artillery service. The weapon gave a number of advantages:

- The ability to fire at high trajectory made the selection of gun positions easier. A clear field of fire was not necessary, allowing the howitzer to be positioned under the cover of trees or buildings; a distinct advantage when fighting a rapidly changing mobile war on a battlefield.
- When compared to a field gun, the propelling charge used for the howitzer could be varied to a far greater degree. Subsequently, the variable trajectory allowed a much wider range of firing missions.
- Due to the heavier ammunition fired by the howitzer, the destructive impact on a target was more significant.

However, the howitzer had a much lower muzzle velocity which made the type of limited use as an anti-tank gun. This caused little concern during the early campaigns of the war, but the surprise appearance on the battlefront of the Soviet T-34 medium and KV heavy tanks caused much consternation for the German invaders.

In 1930, Rheinmetall completed the development of the 10.5cm leFH 18 and deliveries to the artillery began in 1935: By 1 September 1939, more than 4,800 had been delivered.

10.5cm leFH 18

Calibre	10.5cm
Weight (travelling)	3,030kg
Weight (ready to fire)	2,250kg
Range (maximum)	10,600m
Range (effective)	4,000 to 8,000m
Rate of fire	6rpm
Muzzle velocity	471mps
Able to fire gas/smoke	yes
Transport	Horse or vehicle towed

The wheels on 10.5cm leFH 18 issued to tank or motorized infantry divisions were fitted with solid rubber tyres for towing by a motor vehicle.

The crew of a 10.5cm leFH 18 practice gun drill. After adjusting the gun sight, K1 (the gunner) gunner has stepped away, as K2 prepares to pull the firing lanyard. Note the recoil spades have not been dug which requires two of the crew to hold them. The gun limber is parked adjacent to the gun.

A new heavy field howitzer was developed at the same time as the leFH 18, which was to be manufactured by Rheinmetall. The 15cm *schwere Feldhaubitze* (sFH – heavy field howitzer) 18 entered service with the artillery in 1935, and a total of 2,408 had been delivered by September 1939.

As with the *lang* (long) sFH 16, the new gun was intended to be deployed against soft targets.

A battery of 15cm sFH 18 (motorized) prepare to fire. The four guns are positioned near adjacent to a road allowing the half-track tractors to be easily moved to the cover of tree and bushes.

15cm sFH 18

Calibre	15cm
Weight (travelling)	6,304kg
Weight (ready to fire)	5,512kg
Range (maximum)	13,500m
Range (effective)	3,000 to 12,000m
Rate of fire	4rpm
Muzzle velocity	471mps
Able to fire gas/smoke	Yes
Transport	Vehicle towed

The requirement for a new long-range field gun to replace the 10cm K 17 led to the development of a more powerful weapon. A 10.5cm barrel was mounted on the carriage 15cm sFH 18 and a number of other parts from the gun were also utilized. The gun was designated *schwere* 10cm *Kanone* (s 10cm K – heavy 10cm cannon) 18. The s 10cm K 18 was deployed against the same type of target as the K 17. By September 1939, a total of 402 had been delivered to the military.

The s 10 K 18 and the 15cm sFH 18 used the same carriage. When a team of horses was used, the gun barrel and the carriage would be transported in two separate loads to reduce weight. Here the barrel of a s 10cm K 18 is being manhandled on to a *Rohrwagen* (barrel wagon).

s 10cm K 18	
Calibre	15cm
Weight in (travelling)	5,642kg
Weight (ready to fire)	5,284kg
Range (maximum)	18,500m
Range (effective)	5,000 to 18,000m
Rate of fire (maximum)	4rpm
Muzzle velocity	835mps
Able to fire gas/smoke	No
Transport	Vehicle towed

2

MOBILITY FOR THE ARTILLERY

The introduction of more artillery pieces into military service brought with it many logistical and transport problems as teams of horses were used to haul the weapons. Each light gun used by the foot artillery and horse artillery was usually drawn by a team of four or six horses with more required to haul the field carts used to carry the crew, ammunition and other equipment. Over a period of time, the term *Feldartillerie* (field artillery) became the standard nomenclature used by the Imperial German Army.

The foot artillery element of the Imperial German Army was also deployed to provide coastal and fortress defences and later become part of the *schwere Artillerie* (heavy artillery).

During the 1800s, the foot artillery and the more mobile horse artillery would, in general, be capable of meeting the tactical demands of most conflicts being fought at that time. Teams of horses were the usual motive power to move guns into new firing positions and also to replenish ammunition and general supplies. In most instances the foot (or field) artillery would be able to keep pace with the infantry units when pursuing a retreating enemy.

Initially items of heavy artillery were not deployed in large numbers on the battlefield, as many were mounted in static emplacements such as coastal defences. However this would change when many European nations began to build defensive fortresses along their borders. After the being defeated in the Franco-Prussian War (1870 to 1871), France began building a number of these structures at places of strategic importance along her eastern borders. As time progressed the fortresses were continually improved and the armament upgraded to present what military planners envisaged as an impregnable barrier to any future invader. To attack and defeat such heavily constructed and armed fortifications, new types of heavy artillery capable of firing massively powerful

The 7.7cm FlaK manufactured by Rheinmetall was one of the first anti-aircraft (AA) guns to be mounted on the load bed of a truck.

The Krupp-built 8.8cm FlaK 16 was transported on a two-axle trailer. Unlike the later FlaK 18, it was usually fired from the trailer after two outriggers were lowered to stabilize the platform.

ammunition would be required. Military planners in many countries began to issue specifications for these heavy and super-heavy guns and for shells filled with the newly developed high explosives. Once a fortress had been defeated, the guns of the heavy artillery could then be deployed to support the infantry and other forces as they continued their advance.

At the outbreak of World War I, many of these weapons remained in service, but the military continued to strive for the development of longer-range guns firing heavier shells. However this increase in firepower came with an increase in weight to a point where teams of horses could no longer be used to tow the weapons. Military planners now faced a new challenge: find a suitable method of traction.

The transportation problem was partially solved by mounting a heavy gun on a railway wagon to take advantage of the ever-growing rail system in Europe, but although this was a 'solution' it did have many limitations. The age of mechanized transport was approaching.

To meet requirements on the battlefront, the German Imperial Army specified the development of two types of heavy gun. For *Steilfeuer* (high trajectory fire), 15cm and 21cm were introduced, with 10cm, 13cm and also a 15cm for heavy *Flachfeuer* (flat trajectory fire).

In 1900, the standard type for the German heavy artillery, the *schwere Feldhaubitze* (sFH – heavy field howitzer) entered service. Initially Krupp was contracted to develop the 15cm sFH 93 which weighed 2,235kg and had a range of 6,000m. The gun was of conventional construction and drawn by a team of horses.

To improve transportation, Krupp soon began the development of the 15cm sFH 02 which weighed 2,035kg and had an improved range of 7,000m. The army now had a gun which could now keep pace with the infantry.

By the autumn of 1914 the fighting had come to a halt and the many years of trench warfare had begun. In an attempt to break the impasse, German military planners ordered a number of 15cm naval guns to be sent to positions in the battle area (see report below). The gun, manufactured by Krupp, had a maximum range of 19km and was mounted on simple box-type wheeled carriage and designated 15cm *Schnellfeuerkanone* (rapid fire cannon) on *Räderlafette* (wheeled carriage). The gun was broken down into three loads – gun barrel, carriage and a turntable-type mounting – to facilitate transport.

The movement of the 21cm high-trajectory gun – a heavy weapon that was vital for any attack on a fortress or a heavily fortified system of bunkers – would prove to be a serious challenge. Like other heavy weapons the solution was to transport the barrel and the gun carriage as separate loads. In heavy mud (common in autumn and winter) the rim of each wheel would be fitted with rectangular plates to prevent sinking, and bundles of wood (fascines) would be carried to fill in ditches or areas of very deep mud. Although a gun battery would be the strengthened it did require a significant amount of time and involved large numbers of men, horses and other material.

The introduction into service of heavy flat trajectory guns would follow, but not at the same pace. A report written at the beginning of World War I showed that the lack of this type of gun was most sorely felt by German artillery forces. During mobilization only one battalion with four batteries equipped with the

The Daimler KD 1, an all-wheel-drive vehicle, was normally used to tow the 8.8cm FlaK 16. The gun crew was carried in the truck and on the trailer. A shortage of materials meant that both had to be fitted with steel-rimmed wheels.

10cm K 04 and a further eight batteries equipped with the 13cm K 08 were available. The artillery urgently required a more effective 15cm weapon and this would be developed as the war drew on.

In the early 1900s, many breeders in Germany intensified their attempts to produce a draught horse strong enough to haul a heavy payload. One such breed was the *Rheinisch Deutsches Kaltblut* (Rhenish German Coldblood), an extremely strong and reliable horse which could have a working life of up to 20 years: a team of four in harness would be used to move a 15cm sFH.

Beginning of Mechanization

At the time of the Franco-Prussian War, steam-powered traction engines were becoming more available, and contemporary reports note that this type of vehicle had been successfully used to tow artillery and ammunition carriers. Despite the traction engine being seen as a valuable asset, very few were used during the conflict and development did not continue during the short period of peace before World War I.

A possible further reason was the negative attitude taken by many of the ageing leaders of the Imperial German Army who showed their distinct aversion to technical progress – a backward attitude when building a modern military.

Which type of motive power should be chosen; steam or the petrol/paraffin [oil] engine or petrol-electric propulsion? Each had its own benefits and drawbacks but none were actively evaluated by the military.

In 1917, Daimler-Motoren-Gesellschaft delivered some 981 of their Daimler KD 1 to the military to tow the 15cm K 16 and 7.7cm and 8.8cm FlaK. The KD 1 was powered by a 100hp engine and had a top speed of 35kph on surfaced roads. It was sometimes referred to as *Sonderkraftfahrzeug* (SdKfz – special-purpose motor vehicle) 1.

However in 1900, the Prussian war ministry decided to establish a commission with the sole task of evaluating a number of efficient powered vehicles which were at that time available to civilian customers in the Reich.

- Trucks of various horsepower performance and cargo-carrying capacity for the transportation of materials quickly and economically.
- Road tractor units capable of hauling a heavy load (gun).

It was thought that a vehicle would be more efficient than a team of horses in terms of speed and load carrying, but it had to be accepted that a vehicle would lack of off-road mobility.

A short time after the beginning of World War I, the question of transport to the battlefront gained more significance, particularly for moving the heavy guns which exceeded the weight of earlier weapons.

An informative report from *Fußartillerie Regiment* 16 (foot artillery regiment 16) details the mobility problems experienced by a heavy artillery unit. In 1915, the regiment and two other batteries were each supplied with two ex-naval 15cm *Schnellfeuerkanone* in *Räderlafette*:

The A7V *Überlandwagen* (cross-country vehicle) utilized the chassis and engine from the first German-built tank and was normally used to transport supplies. An unknown number were mounted with two captured Russian 76.2mm anti-aircraft (AA) guns thus creating a self-propelled gun.

A battery of 10.5cm leFH 18 guns towed by le ZgKw 3t (SdKfz 11) are paraded before Adolf Hitler on the occasion of his birthday. At that time, the German half-track tractors provided the artillery with previously unknown high mobility on paved roads and rough terrain.

When issued to a motorized artillery regiment, the 15cm sFH 18 would be towed by a m ZgKw 8t (SdKfz 7).

On 23 June 1915, the 5th Batterie/Fußartillerie Regiment 16 accepted two 15cm SK in *Radlafette* from the Krupp factory in Essen. Two steam-powered ploughing engines and five petrol-engined tractors were delivered from the *Zugmaschinenpark* (tractor facility) at Opladen. The first driving trial was undertaken together with 56 heavy horses. During the trial four of the petrol-engined and one steam-powered tractor failed and all had to be returned to Opladen for major overhaul. Replacement tractors were not available. Since the battery was to be transported to the western front immediately, a further 20 horses were supplied. The next trial was with harnessed horses and this ended successfully. Although the horses were in poor condition due to being underfed, they proved to be reliable and willing. However, the horses which had been harnessed to the gun carriage and the limber became exhausted very quickly. Each gun barrel was towed by ten horses, resulting in the team being some 30m long. Each cart used to transport parts of the mounting weighted 9,145kg, but due to the better weight distribution only six horses were required.

The report identifies the many problems associated with delivering these heavy guns to the frontline; many narrow roads which passed through small villages could be impassable and often required the removal of telegraph poles and roadside trees. In their first deployment on the western front, the above unit took four hours to march 12km on a firm straight road. In July, the unit was transported to the Eastern Front where it would be faced with even poorer road conditions; one march took nearly 14 hours to cover 10km of mud-covered track. A planned crossing of the river Vistula was carried through using a newly built bridge, but the 15cm guns were too heavy and had to be sent to a ferry crossing (4.5km in 5 hours). Gun No.2 was loaded on a pontoon, but as the gun was being positioned it slipped off and fell into the water, killing two of the crew. It took three hours to load, cross and unload Gun No.1. The march to the firing position over the flood plain took more than 10 hours and required 24 horses, with assistance from numerous gunners hauling traces. When the gun was finally in position and ready to open fire, the Russian forces had abandoned their positions and moved out. Subsequently not one shot was fired.

A salvage team had recovered Gun No.2 from the river and it was returned in time for when the battery moved to Eydtkuhnen [Chernyshevskoye] in East Prussia. The battery commander was ordered to move the guns with some urgency and requested the assistance of heavy road tractors, but they became bogged down in deep sand and were unable to reach the guns. As a solution he commandeered 56 horses from other units, allowing each gun to be towed by 28 horses, assisted by 80 men hauling on the harness traces. The return march to the ferry crossing took 6½ hours, and the river crossing a further 9 hours. On the way to the railway station at Kozienice a small stream had to be crossed, but the bridge was too narrow and the guns had to be hauled across the soft river bed. This required 40 horses for each gun and another 20 harnessed to the gun limber. During this forced march six horses became totally exhausted and died.

Heavy artillery such as the 24cm K3 had to be transported as separate loads on articulated trailers. This *Rohrwagen* (barrel wagon) is attached to an s ZgKw 18t (SdKfz 9). Visible behind the barrel wagon is another carrying the massive breech block.

After the fall of the fortress at Grodno [Hrodna], the battery was transferred south into Hungary, where it was to support 11.Armee for the crossing of the Danube for the invasion of Serbia. Initially their approach to the pre-prepared gun position began without any problems, but heavy rain turned the clay-surfaced road into a quagmire of rutted cloying mud. Steering the steam-powered tractor became impossible and despite fitting mud chains the drive wheels were devoid of grip. To assist, the crews laboured to collect dry bracken and straw to place under the wheels, while others fixed ropes to the sides of the wagons to prevent them from slipping off the road: all too frequently their efforts failed. Later in the night, the unit harnessed four horses to the front of each tractor to help keep the vehicle in the middle of the muddy track. The march was for a distance of 13km which was covered in 4½ hours by the horse-drawn wagons and 13 hours by the tractors towing the guns. But, as soon as the battery reached its pre-prepared position, orders were received for the unit to move some 38km to a new gun site. The march had to be carried out during the hours of darkness, but the weather was dry and the clay road surface hard allowing unhindered running. However, every 90 minutes the steam tractors had to halt and be replenished with coal and the boiler filled with water. The steam-powered tractors required 13 hours to complete the march, while the horse-drawn transport only required 5 hours.

After a successful deployment, the battery was ordered to march to the nearest railway station and prepare for shipment north to Courland [Kurzeme]. The previous long marches had caused serious damage to the transmissions on the steam-powered tractors requiring them to be returned to the maintenance facility at Opladen, Leverkusen, Germany.

The report concludes with the remark that the horse proved to be far more effective and reliable in difficult terrain than the steam-powered tractor. However in 1917, the unit was reorganized and renamed as the 3./Battalion 144 and at the same time was issued with new 15cm K 16. Also in 1917, Daimler-Motoren-Gesellschaft (DMG) began to deliveries of their KDI 100 all-wheel-drive artillery tractor to the army where it was used to tow the new and 5,080kg-lighter artillery piece.

Early Self-propelled Guns

Towards the end of World War I, an increasing number of reliable motor vehicles were being delivered to the military of both sides and many were adapted. Some had a light field gun mounted on the load bed, and many were converted as mobile anti-aircraft artillery.

A most interesting approach was the mounting of two 7.62cm K-FlaK 18 on the load bed of an *Überlandwagen* – a fully tracked carrier using the suspension of the A7V tank.

The Half-track Tractor

In the latter years of World War I, British and Allied forces began to use increasing numbers of all types of motor vehicle for an ever-increasing range of duties, but German forces continued to rely mainly on horse-drawn transport, particularly for the artillery. However, by the end of the war the general staff of the Imperial Army had finally accepted that the motor vehicle was a valuable military asset and also that German manufacturers were ready to deliver. But in 1919, when the *Reichswehr* was established, Germany was faced with the severe reparations placed on it by the Treaty of Versailles which restricted funds, especially for military purposes.

An important milestone was reached in 1905 when the British company Hornsby of Grantham patented their design for a continuous track. The British Army was quick to recognize the value of this invention and ordered the building of a number of artillery tractors. These fully tracked vehicles were then trialled over all types of rough terrain and many ground conditions.

When Adolf Hitler seized power on 30 January 1933, the process of Germany regaining its military sovereignty began and with it came the investment in specialized military equipment. Even before the *Wehrmacht* was formed

When first produced 1935, the Kraus Maffei KM m 8 was fitted with a 115hp petrol engine, which allowed the vehicle to achieve a top speed of 50kph. The vehicle is finished in *Reichswehr* three-tone camouflage.

in 1935, many important and far-reaching decisions had been made for the Germany military of the future. Firstly passenger cars and trucks – most had two-wheel drive – that were built for the civilian market were delivered to the military. One of the first specialized developments was the *Halbketten Zugmaschine* (half-track prime mover), a vehicle designed to combine high road speeds with excellent off-road mobility. The type was built in a range of sizes from 1,016kg to 18,289kg towing capacity.

At first, limited numbers of halftracks were available and only delivered to artillery formations attached to tank divisions and also the light divisions. As production of the type caught up with requirements, deliveries began to even more artillery units. But in 1939, there was still a shortage of the type (as there would be throughout the war) as the equipping process continued, leaving many tank units and virtually all the infantry divisions dependent on the horse to haul equipment and supplies.

Self-propelled Guns for the *Panzertruppe*

In 1932, military manoeuvres were carried out on the training areas at Jüterbog and Grafenwöhr with the objective of evaluating how to conduct a mobile war. At that time it was an idea in the minds of Guderian and Lutz, two of the few forward-looking officers in the German *Panzertruppe*. The lack of actual equipment required the use of dummy vehicles to replicate tanks and other armoured vehicles.

A le ZgKw 3t (SdKfz 11) from 13.PzDiv tows a 10.5cm leFH 18 during the initial phase of *Unternehmen* (operation) Barbarossa in 1941. According to a number of after-action reports, the SdKfz 11 lacked sufficient ground clearance.

The purpose of the exercise:

a) Clarification of opinions regarding the tactical use of combat cars (tanks).
b) Better tactical defence for combat cars.
c) The cooperation of combat cars with other weapons.
d) Collate the experiences of the leading of armoured formations during the manoeuvres.

A report was compiled and published in September 1932:

> Tanks are solely a weapon for offensive warfare and they will seek to defeat the target at the focal point of an attack. All other weapons must provide support for this action.
>   Due to their strong firepower, high mobility and ability to break through enemy lines, our tank units must operate independently in combat. Slower weapons must advance at their own pace, so as not to thwart any advantages gained by tank forces.

For the artillery, the last paragraph would have serious consequences due to its role of providing support for all combat units, but now fundamental change was in the air.

For the constantly under-funded conventional infantry division all the disadvantages of their slow-moving, horse-drawn artillery had to be accepted, but not by the highly mobile Panzer and motorized infantry divisions.

After the *Anschluss*, the annexation of Austria, weapons used by the Austrian army became available to the German army, including the 42cm Mörser M 17. Like many other heavy guns it had to be moved as separate loads. Here a *Rohrwagen* is hitched to an Austro-Daimler *Artillerie-Generatorwagen* M.16, which generated electric power to drive the trailer. The vehicles were later replaced by s ZgKw 18t (SdKfz 9).

A 15cm sFH 18 heavy field gun carefully covered with protective tarpaulins is attached to an early Krauss-Maffei m9 (SdKfz 7). Note the wicker matting, to be placed under the wheels of the gun, stacked in the back of the tractor unit.

German military planners were constantly made aware of these shortcomings. On a purely organizational level, the first Panzer divisions were to receive a tank brigade which would, with certain limitations, operate independently against targets with the objective of making the breakthrough. The other divisional units, including the artillery regiment, would follow up as quickly as possible.

The report continues:

> Faced with a possible attack by enemy tanks, the artillery will undertake two missions.
> - The long and medium-range attack on enemy assembly areas, also being ready to attack the initial advance by enemy tanks.
> - Destruction by direct fire of enemy armour which has made a breakthrough.

This is not surprising. Firstly, the artillery element of the tank division must always be adjacent or in close proximity. Secondly, the artillery battalion should be able to follow the advance or, even better, be equipped for mobile warfare. For all other attached sections the report continues:

> The infantry units [*Schützenbrigade* in a Panzer division] attached to the tank unit must be able to closely follow the advance. During an attack, the infantry must also not be hindered by (slower) heavy weapons.

Conversely, if the infantry guns of the *Schützenbrigade* (rifle brigade) or those of the field artillery are to be in front-line positions, their mobility has to be decisively increased.

In the coming years much consideration was given to improve and increase mobility for the artillery elements in tank divisions and also motorized infantry divisions.

In August 1935, a significant exercise organized by 1.PzDiv was conducted on the training grounds at Munster.

A report on the event was published on 24 December 1935:

> The basic rule for establishing an artillery unit in a Panzer division is to give the commander of the division sole responsibility for an artillery regiment. Tactical orders are to be issued by the [artillery] regiment commander, or split between the commanders of the tank brigade and/or the motorized infantry.
>
> To represent a tank brigade in combat during the exercises, one of the two artillery battalions was to be provided with self-propelled guns. During the exercises, only one battalion (horse drawn) was available, the other was represented by machine-gun armed tanks [PzKpfw I]. Both battalions were attached to the motorized rifle and the tank brigade.

During the rapidly increasing pace of the (mock) battles, it proved impossible to gather exact statistics for the possible deployment of a self-propelled gun battalion in combat.

Principally, the missions presented to motorized artillery are comparable to those for towed artillery units in an infantry division. However, it must be demanded that ready to fire preparations must be made quicker and a change of position to be achieved more rapidly.

Any mission directed by the Panzer brigade to the supporting artillery cannot be fulfilled by horse-drawn units. After a successful breakthrough, the horse-drawn artillery is too slow in getting into position which significantly reduces their ability to open supporting fire.

Any artillery support for the Panzer brigade requires it to have the ability to immediately follow the tank advance, also the type must have high mobility over all terrain and protection against enemy fire: an armoured fully tracked vehicle mounting an artillery piece.

Furthermore it must be decided, as to whether this vehicle will be armed with a 7.5cm or 10.5cm gun. Trials using both weapons will have to be conducted in the near future. A

When first issued to the Panzer divisions, the 15cm sIG 33 heavy infantry gun was normally towed by a le ZgKw 1t (SdKfz 10), but here one is hitched to the more powerful SdKfz 11.

10.5cm gun will have a greater impact in the target, but inevitably will make the vehicle heavier and give it a conspicuous superstructure. Due to the size of the gun ammunition storage will be considerably limited.

Until trials with 10.5cm self-propelled guns have been completed, the tank brigade will have to continue to use the 7.5cm-armed tanks of the heavy companies [PzKpfw IV]. The crews will have to be trained on how to use this weapon as artillery. Other than supporting light tank units to achieve a breakthrough, the heavier tanks must occasionally be able to eliminate enemy observation posts and anti-tank gun positions from behind cover, and also to fire smoke.

However, staff at the headquarters of the *Panzertruppe* complained that the heavy Panzer companies must not be overstretched and stated that it was now imperative to create a battalion of armoured self-propelled support artillery.

An SdKfz 11 from 5.SS PzGrenDiv Wiking hauls a 15cm sIG 33 heavy infantry gun through the thick mud during the *Rasputitsa* (mud season) in Russia. The breech block and muzzle are covered to protect the gun from rain and mud.

But the above was impossible to realize in 1935, as were many other requirements, due to severe budgetary constraints. Even the PzKpfw IV *Begleitwagen* (support vehicle), mounting a short-barrelled 7.5cm KwK L/24 gun, had not entered production.

One of the many proposed organizational structures for the future Panzer division was published in September 1934.

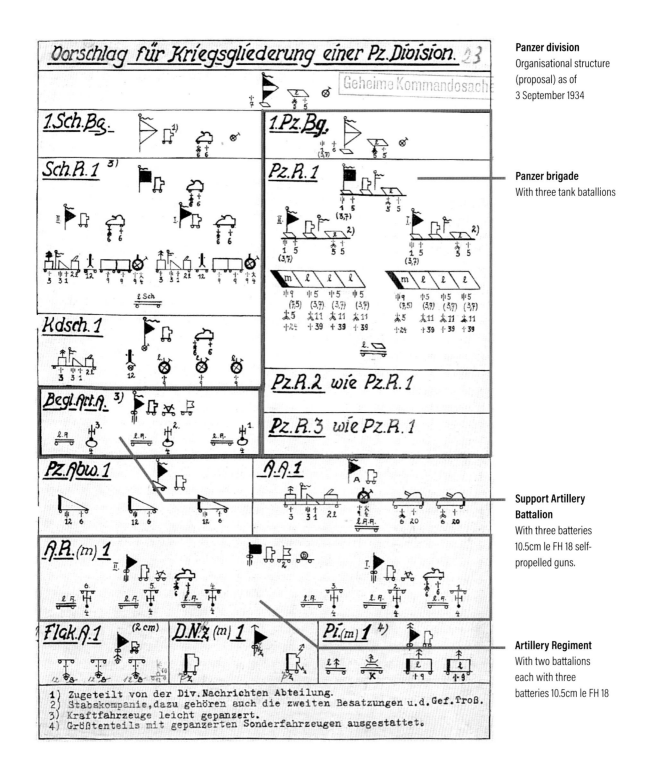

Panzer division
Organisational structure
(proposal) as of
3 September 1934

Panzer brigade
With three tank batallions

**Support Artillery
Battalion**
With three batteries
10.5cm le FH 18 self-
propelled guns.

Artillery Regiment
With two battalions
each with three
batteries 10.5cm le FH 18

German half-track tractors were originally designed to travel at high average speeds on paved roads and also retain mobility over rough terrain. This s ZgKw 5t has been positioned over a ditch to illustrate the flexibility of its suspension.

A Panzer brigade was formed of three tank regiments, and the artillery elements were a *mittlere Artillerie-Regiment* (m ArtRegt – medium artillery regiment) made up of six batteries of 10.5cm leFH 18 (mot). A further *Begleit-Artillerie-Abteilung* (support artillery battalion) was to be equipped with 12 10.5cm leFH 18 (mot). Later in the war, Erich von Manstein followed this practice and demanded that *Sturmgeschütz Abteilungen* (StuGAbt – assault gun battalions) must be issued to infantry divisions.

However this trial organizational structure was never realized, but it does indicate the direction in which the creators of the Panzer divisions were moving. The constant shortages of material and limited funding did not allow many of these innovative concepts to be realized.

Mobile Artillery for the Infantry Divisions

As previously noted, when the first wave of infantry divisions were formed all were to be issued with horse-drawn artillery. However, the important role proposed for the new Panzer divisions would also require an infantry involvement. Despite the fact that the Panzer divisions had a strong infantry element (a fully motorized *Schützenregiment*) the *Oberkommando des Heeres* (OKH – army high command) even requested mobile infantry divisions. In May 1936, four divisions were earmarked for being transferred to *Infanteriedivision* (mot) (InfDiv – infantry division [motorized]) and the chosen units were 2.Div, 13.Div and 29.Div.

The planned motorized units included:

a) Complete artillery elements
b) Engineer elements
c) Signals elements

The motorization of the infantry for each division and all other combat support elements would be addressed at the beginning of 1937.

The OKH document shows that the transformation of an InfDiv into a InfDiv (mot) as a straightforward possibility. Two key details are noted:

- A normal infantry division requires 1,120 motor vehicles, the proposed motorized infantry division will require 3,440.
- The combined fuel consumption will increase from 32,000 litres to 106,000 litres per 100km.

For comparison, the estimated fuel consumption of a Panzer division was stated to be 150,000 litres per 100km. In autumn 1937, planning began to convert the first four divisions and in anticipation of any problems, it was decided to keep a number of horse-drawn artillery units as a precaution.

The Krauss Maffei m 11 was the most numerous production variant of the SdKfz 7. A shortcoming of the half-track design is being demonstrated: when climbing a slope the front axle would often lift off and if it landed heavily the axle could be damaged.

3

1936–1939 DEFINING THE STANDARDS

In 1939, the programme to re-equip German combat units with the most up-to-date artillery weapons continued apace. The divisions – infantry, motorized infantry, mountain and also tank – had been issued with the latest *Kriegsstärkenachweisung* (KStN – organizational structures) published in 1937: It must be remembered that these structures stated the ideal not the actual target. However, the six waves of infantry divisions established by the end of 1939 (approximately 90) were in general fully equipped according to these structures. However, ever present shortages of equipment meant that older types of gun (many from World War I) had to be issued, even military pattern vehicles were regularly replaced by civilian motor vehicles or trucks.

At the same time, motor transport for the artillery was primarily focused on the motorized infantry and tank divisions. Also the heavy artillery organized at *Heeresgruppen* (army group) would also be given priority.

Infantry Divisions

The German artillery elements in the infantry divisions had to rely on teams of horses to move their guns. The divisional artillery regiments consisted of four batteries, of which three were issued with four 10.5cm leFH 18 each – a number of units, were issued with the older 10.5cm leFH 16 – the fourth battery was normally issued with four 15cm sFH 18, but some units had still the 15cm sFH 13 in their inventory).

The 13.Kp in each of the three infantry regiments was the *Infanteriegeschütz-Kompanie* (InfGeschKp – assault gun company) issued with six 7.5cm leIG 18

The only two 10cm K 18 armed PzSfl IVa built were delivered to the artillery school at Jüterbog to undertake firing trials. The vehicle was severely underpowered, being fitted with a 180hp Maybach HL66P – also used to power the PzKpfw II Ausf L *'Luchs'* (lynx) – to drive a vehicle weighing 22,353kg.

light infantry guns and two 15cm sIG 33: the reconnaissance battalion was equipped with two leIG 18. Many divisions were forced to accept a reduced allotment; on a number of occasions delivery was delayed or no heavy infantry guns were issued.

Mountain Divisions

Initially three *Gebirgsdivisionen* (GebDiv – mountain divisions) were formed; 1.GebDiv had three infantry regiments, each of the two others had two. The infantry regiments were equipped with 12 horse-drawn 7.5cm *leichte Gebirgs-Infanterie-Geschütz* (leGeb IG – light mountain infantry gun) 18. The artillery regiment was formed of two battalions equipped with eight horse-drawn 7.5cm *Gebirgs-Geschschütz* (mountain guns) 36, one or two battalions equipped with 12 horse-drawn 10.5cm leFH 18 and a heavy motorized battalion with eight 15cm sFH 18.

Infantry Divisions (mot)

Motorized infantry divisions had two instead of three infantry regiments which, when compared to a conventional infantry division, were equipped with the same number of infantry guns, but all were motorized. The artillery regiment

The 15cm sIG 33 complete with the box-type carriage gun and wheels was, for simplicity, mounted top of a PzKpfw I hull. The lack of space between the superstructure and gun considerably hindered the crew when in action. Note the *Rundblickfernrohr* (Rbl.F) 38 dial-type gun sight.

Three 8.8cm *Bunkerknacker* during the advance in France: the considerable height of the type made it difficult to conceal. The gun commander would always be alert to selecting a safe firing position. Note the crew has fitted wire mesh over the bonnet and gun shield to facilitate the attachment of foliage to camouflage the vehicle.

within the division was also equipped with an identical number of guns and again these were motorized.

Panzer Divisions

These divisions were promoted as the spearhead for the mobile warfare of the future and were to be fully motorized. Principally, the artillery regiment was to be equipped with 24 10.5cm leFH 18 and 12 15cm sFH 18, exactly the same as that in a motorized infantry division. A number of tank divisions (2.PzDiv, 3.PzDiv, 7.PzDiv and 10.PzDiv) were issued with one battery of four s 10cm K 18 for flat trajectory fire, replacing one battery of 15cm sFH 18.

However, the allotment of infantry guns would be different. As noted in a list of KStN documents (for Panzer divisions) dated 1940, the three battalions in a *Schützenregiment* would each be allotted two 15cm sIG 33 and four 7.5cm leIG 18, more leIG 18 were to be issued to the machine-gun company and also – if there was one – the *Kradschützen* (motorcycle mounted) reconnaissance company. However, there were always vast discrepancies between what was planned and reality. Organizational structures dated January 1940, note that no 15cm sIG 33 had been issued.

Divisional Artillery

The divisional artillery was expected to fight a wide range of combat missions:

- The light and heavy infantry guns of the infantry regiments would accompany the infantry and be prepared to attack and defeat soft and semi-hard targets at short and medium range. On the defensive they must attempt to destroy any enemy heavy weapons attacking our forces.
- The field artillery, 10.5cm and 15cm howitzers should support the attack by our infantry or tank division at medium and long ranges.
- When available, the s 10cm K 18 and the 8.8cm FlaK 18 (anti-aircraft artillery) heavy field guns, which have a flat trajectory, will be used against long-range targets. Also due to their higher muzzle velocity and better accuracy these guns must, where possible, attempt to combat enemy tanks. These weapons have also proven to be deadly for destroying concrete bunkers and other border fortifications.
- The *Sturmartillerie* [assault artillery] provided another tactical advantage. Their *Sturmgeschütz* [StuG] provided direct close-support fire for our attacking infantry and motorized infantry divisions. Initially it was planned to provide one battalion equipped with 18 StuG to each division.

The *Betonknacker* (concrete buster) was an enormous vehicle and highly effective for attacking enemy pill boxes and other reinforced positions. But the type had poor armour protection for the crew; consequently the commander had to carefully assess the situation before making an attack.

Self-propelled Guns in Combat

In the years leading up to World War II, many high-level meetings were convened in an attempt to decide on how to build a highly mobile artillery and anti-tank gun force. General Lutz and, as he was then, *Oberst* Guderian as the proponents of modern mechanized warfare were convinced that a mobile artillery could be an essential element for their Panzer divisions.

In 1938, planning began to establish the *Schnelle Truppen* (rapid formations) which later became the *Panzertruppen*. The artillery elements in Panzer divisions were from the beginning totally motorized, being equipped with half-track tractors.

However, the *Waffenamt* (WA – ordnance department) had also been discussing the idea of self-propelled artillery since the early 1930s, sometimes with great enthusiasm and others great apathy.

These excerpts from a dissertation published in a German technical magazine dated 1943 give a vivid impression on the dynamic development during establishment of the German armed forces:

Among the most important members on the staff of General Lutz at that time was *Oberst* Guderian, chief of the *Inspektion der Kraftfahrtruppen* [the forerunner of the *Inspektion der Panzertruppen*]. This dedicated officer worked tirelessly and intelligently for the creation of the Panzer divisions. These units designed for rapid and mobile warfare were to be motorized and armoured on all levels. It was from this that the idea of introducing self-propelled guns emerged. An artillery weapon requires a gun mounting as a counterweight to neutralize recoil forces. The weight of the mounting ensures the stability of the gun on the ground, but when the gun is mounted on a vehicle this weight will cause problems with mobility. Before an artillery piece can be manoeuvred into the firing position, it has to be uncoupled from its transport, losing precious time. The crew then has to turn the gun towards the target, while the transport has to be taken to a safe location: the gun and crew is separated from any means of rapid movement. Furthermore, their transport is vulnerable to enemy fire and losses are inevitable.

When Guderian promoted his idea of providing the artillery with full mobility, he was met with staunch resistance. His opponents did not accept that weapons which enabled troops to fight a continuing battle would ever be required. Guderian had recognized that any war of the future would also rely on the tank supported by aircraft. He argued that it was only logical that any artillery units involved in this type of warfare should be held at permanent readiness. Every unit or single gun must be ready to follow the rapidly advancing Panzer spearhead and always be ready to open fire. Thus it was eminently important for self-propelled guns to be supplied to the artillery and provide the force with rapid mobility: A key element in modern mechanized warfare.

Mobility was a constant problem for artillery units. A horse-drawn *Rohrwagen* carrying the gun barrel of 15cm sFH 18 has sunk down in the mud during the Polish campaign. With no recovery vehicles at hand, the only way to save the gun would be to attach more horses.

15cm sIG *Geschütz* 'B', (gun *Biene* – bee) parked at the side of a road in a French village. The tactical marking indicates that the vehicle is from a self-propelled artillery unit.

The above was written after the disastrous defeat of German forces at Stalingrad; Hitler and his cohorts had drawn the German population into a new era of total war. Perhaps this explains the combative tone in the article. The notion that the development of self-propelled artillery came to fruition solely on the demands of Guderian is somewhat questionable.

However, serious design and development work to mount artillery on tracked vehicles had indeed begun in 1936. As work progressed a number of different types were discussed:

- Flat trajectory weapons
- Anti-tank guns
- Direct support weapons
- Infantry guns
- Field artillery

In July 1940, the *Waffenamt* published an interesting document which details a number of self-propelled gun projects and differentiates between those already finished and those being planned for the future. It is interesting to note that the 8.8cm FlaK auf s ZgKw 12t half-track vehicle is not listed, possibly as it was seen as a temporary solution.

A 15cm sIG 33 auf PzKpfw I with an 'Ausfallflagge' (black cross on yellow ground) flag to indicate that there is a mechanical problem. The vehicle does not carry any divisional or tactical markings, typical of sIG Kp 703 when attached to 2.PzDiv.

Schartenbrecher (gun-slot breaker)

In 1935, German military planners began making preparations for a military conflict in the near future. France, thought to be the most likely adversary, and The Low Countries (Holland and Belgium) had concentrated all their military efforts on a defensive strategy, whereas Germany was pursuing an offensive approach. In 1938, the Reich adopted an increasingly hostile foreign policy, and exerted more pressure on the armaments industry to expand production.

German military planners were aware that among the main obstacles to the new German concept of mobile warfare – soon to be named *Blitzkrieg* (lightning attack) – was a system of fortifications built at strategic positions on the borders of Belgium and France.

They considered conventional towed artillery too slow to be brought into action to attack gun positions, bunkers and pillboxes. Alert to this problem, the planners began to search for a solution. In 1936/37, there were two guns in service which seemed to provide a solution for destroying concrete fortifications, the s 10cm K 18 and the 8.8cm FlaK 18 and both had the high muzzle velocity which was indispensable for high accuracy. However, the search for a chassis able to carry either gun was fraught with technical problems. At that time, the design of both the PzKpfw III and PzKpfw IV was all but completed and production of the two types was already a year behind schedule.

The search ended with the 8.8cm FlaK being mounted on an SdKfz 8 heavy half-track vehicle.

In 1939, an even heavier gun became available when the new 12.8cm FlaK 40 entered production. Subsequently this heavy anti-aircraft gun would also be used in the same manner.

8.8cm FlaK 18

The *schwere Zugkraftwagen* (m ZgKw – heavy tractor) 12t (SdKfz 8) proved to be suitable for mounting the 8.8cm FlaK 18. The crew compartment was removed and the space used for the gun mounting. To give the driver some protection an armoured cab was fitted and the gun shield enlarged and reinforced. No accommodation was provided for the gun crew. In 1938, a total of ten vehicles had been completed and delivered.

10cm K 18

By 1938, Krupp was contracted to design and produce a self-propelled gun on the chassis of a fully tracked vehicle: the project was designated PzSfl IVa. The 10.5cm s K 18 was chosen and modified by using a jacket-type gun mount to enable it to meet the planned specification. The gun was mounted

A sIG 33 loaded on a *Sonderanhänger* (SdAnh – special purpose trailer) 115 which had a load capacity of 15,000kg. The guns were often transported in this way to a new location to avoid wear and tear on the already overloaded chassis. However, these trailers were always in short supply.

above the engine in the centre of the hull from a Krupp-built PzKpfw IV and many other components were utilized, including the eight-wheel running gear. However, the type had 50mm thick frontal armour, 20mm for the sides of the superstructure and 10mm for the rear plate which resulted in the type weighing 22,353kg. By comparison, a current production PzKpfw IV Ausf B had 30mm thick armour and weighed 18,797kg.

Despite being some 4,064kg heavier, the engine chosen for the PzSfl IVa was the 180hp Maybach HL 66 rather than a 265hp Maybach HL 120, the standard power unit for the PzKpfw IV. Possibly, this was because the six-cylinder HL 66 engine was smaller and easier to install in the hull, but the lack of engine power would seriously effect mobility and road speed; only 27kph was possible where the planned maximum speed was 40kph. The PzSfl IVa was scheduled to enter production in the autumn of 1942.

In many after-combat reports the type is called a *Betonknacker* (concrete smasher), but officially it was known as a *Bunkerknacker* (bunker buster) or *Schartenbrecher* (gun-slot breaker).

In January 1939, officials from *Waffenprüfamt* (WaPrüf) 6, the bureau responsible for motorization, held a meeting with engineers from Krupp:

Subject: *Selbstfahrlafetten* [Sfl – self-propelled guns]

Dr Olbrich [WaPrüf 6] opened the meeting with the following question for discussion: When used by the artillery, the type will be far more expensive when compared to separate guns and tractors. Furthermore, a tractor could be used for other duties once the gun has been positioned By contrast a self-propelled gun will be totally neutralized after a direct hit. At present there is a high demand for *Sonderkraftfahrzeuge* [special-purpose vehicles] to defeat bunkers, and there is also an increasing demand for SP guns. For this purpose, it is considered unnecessary to use a high-trajectory gun. In this context, the development of the 12.8cm SP gun has been transferred to Rheinmetall. The development of a 15cm SP gun has been cancelled, since to load a 1.5m long shell which weighs 72kg is considered to be too difficult.

Apparently certain members of the *Waffenamt* rejected the necessity of SP guns for the conventional field artillery, pointing to the advantages to having separate heavy towing tractors. Once a tractor had towed a gun into position it was feasible for it to be used for other duties. However, this was the view of a civilian from the department who was always seeking the most effective way for equipment to be used. But in reality on the battlefield, the tractor unit had to be kept in close proximity to the gun to enable a quick change of position; a fact that was made obvious before the war. Any delay could lead to the loss of a gun or even an entire battery if it had been spotted by enemy observers.

It appears that a significant part of the meeting was on the subject of self-propelled guns capable of destroying concrete bunkers and other fortifications. At the time of the meeting, the 10.5cm version was in production and a heavier version armed with a 12.8cm gun is mentioned. A further vehicle armed with a 15cm gun had been proposed but this was rejected by Olbrich. He reasoned that the size and weight of the one-piece (cartridge-type) ammunition originally specified was too cumbersome to be loaded by one man.

12.8cm K L/61

At around the same time, design work commenced on another type of self-propelled gun called *schwerer Betonknacker*. The type was to be armed with

a modified version of the recently developed 12.8cm FlaK 40 which was manufactured by Rheinmetall.

Henschel was contracted to design the hull and running gear and planned to utilize a number of components from their VK 30.01(H) (*Vollkette* – fully-tracked experimental vehicle), the prototype for the *Durchbruchswagen* (DW – breakthrough vehicle) 2. The 12.8cm *Kanone* L/61 was mounted on the top of a considerably lengthened hull with the chosen engine, a 310hp Maybach HL 116, mounted in the centre.

The complete vehicle weighed 37,086kg (the gun weighed over 7,112kg) and was considerably underpowered resulting in a maximum speed of only 25kph.

The vehicle was designated PzSfl V and was expected to enter service in the summer of 1943.

A complete *schwere Artillerie-Abteilung: motorisiert* (s ArtAbt [mot] – heavy artillery battalion: motorized) on the parade ground at their garrison. The guns of two 15cm sFH 18-armed batteries have been positioned facing each other; to the right is a battery of four s 10cm K 18.

Both types of *Betonknacker* were developed for attacking a specific type of target and large-scale production was not planned, so there would not be any new types in the future.

Anti-tank Guns
4.7cm PaK(t)

Long before planned invasion of France it was known that German formations were severely short of medium anti-tank guns. To overcome the problem military planners decided, at the end of 1939, to mount a Czech-built 4.7cm anti-tank gun on a factory-refurbished chassis of obsolete PzKpfw I tanks. A simple but effective solution that provided the *Panzerjägertruppe* (tank destroyer force) with a mobile anti-tank weapon which had better armour-piercing performance than the standard 3.7cm PaK. The 4.7cm PaK(t) auf PzKpfw I was issued to four independent tank destroyer battalions in 1940, and all were involved in the French campaign.

The development and operational history of this self-propelled gun (and others) is covered in *Panzerjäger* Volume I (Osprey 2018).

Direct Support Weapons
Sturmgeschütz

As other self-propelled weapons were being designed and developed, a fully armoured self-propelled gun, the *Sturmgeschütz* (StuG – assault gun) was designed on the initiative of the General of the Infantry Erich von Manstein. The *Sturmgeschütz* was intended to provide close support the infantry as they advanced. The StuG was built using the hull of a PzKpfw III and mounted a 7.5cm *Sturmkanone* (StuK – assault gun) L/24 gun. The StuG entered service in 1940 with the assault battalions of the artillery.

Development and operational history of the assault gun units in *Wehrmacht* service is covered in *Sturmartillerie* (Osprey 2016) and *Sturmgeschütz* (Osprey 2017).

At the same time as the StuG entered front-line service, the *Waffenamt* ordered the development of a *schwerer Panzerjäger* (heavy tank hunter); an unusually far-sighted decision. The specification stated that the vehicle was to mount an 8.8cm KwK L/56 gun, have a combat weight of some 22,353kg and should be based on the hull of a PzKpfw III or PzKpfw IV. Also the type was to fulfill a number of roles – heavy tank destroyer, an assault gun and light *Betonknacker*. It was planned for the type to enter production in autumn 1943, but this did not happen.

It is possible that the planned vehicle was a true replacement for the 8.8cm

FlaK auf s ZgKw 12t (SdKfz 8), but details of its design are not known and the *Waffenamt* responsible for this interesting concept did not pursue it any further. By the time the *Jagdpanther* entered service in 1944, the requirement for attacking concrete fortifications had been transferred to *Sturmpanzer* (assault tank) units.

Infantry Guns
15cm sIG 33

In 1939, the first steps were taken to improve mobility for the artillery elements in a tank division. The heavy 15cm sIG 33 gun, in service with the 13.Kp of a *Schützenregiment*, was selected be mounted on a fully tracked chassis. A *Waffenamt* document states that the type was to be deployed against soft targets.

The original specification called for the gun to be mounted on the chassis of a new type of reconnaissance tank which, at the time, was at the planning stage. The vehicle was to have 50mm thick frontal armour with 20mm on the sides and a combat-ready weight of some 12,193kg. It was expected for the vehicle to have a top speed of 67kph.

A requirement in the original specification is most interesting; the gun must easily be dismountable from the chassis. This allowed the gun to be quickly moved over hard-surfaced roads while saving the tracked chassis from unnecessary wear. The *Waffenamt* expected the type to be ready for production by the autumn of 1942.

However, the specification could not be met. As a solution refurbished PzKpfw I Ausf B chassis were to be used in place of that of the proposed reconnaissance tank. To simplify the modifications to mount a complete 15cm sIG 33 infantry gun, only the front part of the superstructure was removed: otherwise the vehicle was virtually unchanged.

The gun was fitted with a high box-like armoured superstructure which only gave the crew protection against rifle or machine gun armour-piercing ammunition.

Field Artillery

The field artillery elements in a Panzer division were equipped with 10.5cm leFH 18 and 15cm sFH18 medium to high trajectory howitzers and much thought was given to mounting these guns on fully tracked chassis.

However, only the lighter 10.5cm leFH 18 was selected in 1940 for mounting as a self-propelled gun utilizing a shortened PzKpfw IV hull with only six running wheels.

It is intriguing to note that it was planned for the gun to be mounted in a rotatable turret which made it impossible to dismount. This vehicle was expected to be ready for production by winter 1942/43.

4

INTO POLAND

Self-propelled artillery did not play a major role in the fighting during the Polish campaign, indeed the only unit to use the type was *Panzerabwehr-Abteilung* (PzAbwAbt – tank defence battalion) 8 – in 1938 this designation had begun to be changed from 'defence' to a more accurate definition 'destroyer'. This resulted In a gradual renaming to *Panzerjäger-Abteilung* (PzJgAbt – tank destroyer battalion) to emphasize the offensive ability of the *Wehrmacht*. This particular unit was attached to 8.InfDiv and was a considerably better equipped when compared to other standard *Panzerjäger* (PzJg) units.

A leaflet was published promoting 'mobile 8.8cm FlaK platoons' and included details for the deployment of the heavy FlaK guns modified as *Schartenbrecher* (gun-slot breaker)) for ground combat; their primary role would be to destroy enemy pill-box defences and secondary was to defend against enemy tanks. When supporting an infantry advance the unit would be attached to the infantry regiments, but when faced by an attack by enemy tanks the unit was to be attached to the divisional tank destroyer battalion. When deployed as a *Schartenbrecher*, it was usual to allot an individual vehicle; when faced with the task of halting a concentrated tank assault, the complete platoon of three to four vehicles would be moved to defensive positions in the rear. Troops were constantly reminded that the long range and accuracy of the 8.8cm FlaK must always be used to the best advantage.

In certain aspects the task set for *Schartenbrecher* units is similar to those for the *Sturmgeschütz*, and intended to be implemented by infantry divisions in 1940. However, the effect on a target of the 7.5cm StuK L/24 could not be compared to that of the 8.8cm FlaK. After the French campaign, it is easily understandable as to why there was call for a heavy FlaK gun to be mounted in a StuG; the result would be a very formidable weapon.

The gun barrel of the 10.5cm leFH 18 is at full recoil after firing. Any movement of the gun would require it to be repositioned and re-sighted. It was essential for the crew to dig the recoil spades on the gun carriage trails deep into the ground in order to absorb the forces. A well-trained leFh gun crew could fire up to six rounds per minute.

At the beginning of the invasion of Poland, PzAbwAbt 8 fought with AOK 14 in the southern region of the country. After the campaign *Oberstleutnant* Wassmuth, commander of the unit, delivered a lecture to his non-commissioned officers (NCOs) and other ranks of the *Panzerjägertruppe*:

> On 5 August 1939, the battalion moved out for a special operation in the industrial region of Upper Silesia. Anti-tank positions had been prepared in our assigned sector around Gliwice by the end of August. We all expected that soon we would be advancing across the border to give the Polish a severe beating.
>
> Our unit was assembled as follows:
>
> • Staff and signals platoon
> • 1.Kompanie [Kp – company] with ten 8.8cm FlaK on SdKfz 8
> • 2.Kp with 3.7cm PaK
> • 3.Kp with 3.7cm PaK
> • 4.Kp with 2cm FlaK 30
>
> On 3 September 1939, the battalion finally crossed the border, but during the whole campaign we did not have the good fortune to fulfill our original task – defensive action against a large-scale assault by Polish tanks. We were mainly deployed as an advance force for the division.
>
> Now I will describe a few of our combat experiences.

The 15cm sFH 18 and the 10.5cm leFH 18 formed the backbone of the divisional artillery. While firing a continuous bombardment the gun has sunk deep into the soft ground, leaving the recoil spades barely visible. It would be difficult even for a half-track tractor to recover this gun and that is why all ZgKw were fitted with a recovery winch.

USE OF THE BATTALION AS BLOCKING UNIT:
Every infantry regiment was provided with one 8.8cm FlaK platoon in order to attack enemy strongholds. Initially the battalion followed an infantry regiment deployed to our left. Our first alert was on the afternoon of 1 September, when the unit received orders to guard the left flank of the division against a possible Polish attack on Mokra thus protecting our own artillery positions near Bujaków and also the rear positions of our infantry. In peacetime we carried out continuous training, according to regulation, to deploy as a blocking unit. From this training we knew that a PzAbwAbt must be able to accomplish such missions alone. Thorough training in infantry skills and live-fire with rifles are essential as is practice firing the PaK.
Use of the battalion to reinforce the *Aufklärungs-Abteilung* [AufklAbt – reconnaissance battalion] while holding a bridgehead:
The battalion marched during the night in complete darkness to a new location. Here we positioned our 3.7cm PaK and light machine guns to cover a sector of our frontline.

DEPLOYMENT AS ADVANCE PARTY:
The unit was ordered to move in the direction of Wiślica as an advance party. The bridges over the river Nida were to be taken and bridgehead established at Wiślica. On the way the unit met tanks of 5.PzDiv (18 tanks, one battery 10.5cm leFH 18).
We deployed the following units:

This commander of this 15cm sFH 18 (motorized traction) battery has positioned his guns in a slight depression on an otherwise open field. Ammunition has been piled near to the guns in preparation for opening fire. Two heavy half-track tractors and the transport elements of the ammunition squad are parked nearby.

Staff PzAbwAbt 8
1./PzAbwAbt 8 (nine 8.8cm FlaK)
3./PzAbwAbt 8
3.PiAbt 8 (mot) (motorized engineers)

The battalion was immediately ordered into action. Four of our 8.8cm FlaK guns were positioned on each side of the road being used by our advancing forces, so that they could open fire on enemy positions in the village. The tanks of 5.PzDiv advanced in close formation with 3.PiAbt 8 (mot) to defuse any demolition charges left on the bridges. Concealed enemy machine gun and anti-tank gun positions, supported by heavy artillery fire, delayed the assault. When the firing positions were identified, the 8.8cm guns of I./PzJgAbt 8 knocked out one gun after the other, each with a single round. However, experience has shown that the 3.7cm PaK, when firing the recently introduced high-explosive round, also proved capable of destroying such targets.

This combat has shown that anti-tank units must not only be trained to fight tanks. Importantly, all officers must encourage their NCOs and troopers to think carefully and fight independently.

Above: Getting a 15cm sFH 18 into a firing position was hard work; it required six men to lift the carriage trails and another three to move the limber. The recoil spades would be fitted after the trails had been positioned. A gun crew was expected to perform its work in rain, mud, snow and even in the lowest temperatures.

Left: A 15cm sFH 18 weighed 6,401kg, which allowed it to be towed as one load by a half-tracked tractor. This pre-war photograph shows a 1935-type KM m8 prime mover designated m ZgKw 8t (SdKfz 7).

Other than speaking about German mission-type combat tactics, which proved to be so successful later in the war, he also detailed the advantages of heavy self-propelled artillery. Any enemy position on the battlefront would easily be destroyed by the high-velocity guns firing high-explosive (HE) ammunition.

Work for a horse-drawn 15cm sFH 18 unit was even more strenuous. Part of the crew prepares the gun carriage, while others get the barrel wagon into position to allow the gun barrel to be hauled onto the gun cradle.

The crew of a 10.5cm leFH 18 has commandeered a team of oxen to tow the gun, possibly due to a shortage of horses. The constant lack of heavy tractors, due to the inability of German armaments manufacturers to keep up with demand, forced many infantry divisions to use unconventional forms of transport.

He also identifies the need for continuous training to produce specialized soldiers such as tank destroyers. He continues:

ADVANCE TO THE RIVER SAN, TO ESTABLISH BRIDGEHEADS AT KRESZOV AND ULANÓW:
After the infantry arrived, PzAbwAbt 8 was ordered to assist with establishing a bridgehead at the river, before enemy forces could take up position. During the afternoon, our unit supported I./SS Germania to help them complete the task. During these missions, the battalion was operating 120km ahead of the main elements of the division; their sole purpose was to prepare a crossing over the river San. After advancing over very bad roads they arrived at the river San, only to find that the bridges had already been destroyed by Polish forces. In this situation it was essential to take the opposite bank before enemy forces could dig defensive positions. All of our 8.8cm FlaK engaged and destroyed any pocket of resistance observed. The rapid and accurate fire prepared the ground for I./SS Germania, whose infantry crossed the river and captured the opposite bank: a short time later they entered the city of Ulanów. It was extremely fortunate that Luftwaffe aircraft were available to bomb enemy positions in and around the city. Polish forces (a reinforced battalion) retreated to positions in woodland to the east of Ulanów.

Deployment as Divisional Rapid Task Force at Focal Points:
During the night the battalion received orders to transfer to the south of Narol travelling via Biłgoraj and Tarnogród.
Our units deployed:
PzJgAbt 8
One platoon PiAbt 8
AufklAbt 8 without cavalry troop
14./Infantry Regiment 28

The enemy had made a breakthrough at the southern sector of the Tomaszów Lubelski and Krasnobród pocket, and captured Narol. The only road for supplying 28.InfDiv was now controlled by the enemy. The advance party, assisted by PiAbt 47 (corps troop), received orders to retake Narol. Our 8.8cm FlaK guns were to be the only artillery element. The attack began on time as riflemen from the tank destroyer battalion, assisted by pioneer troops, attacked as infantry. Accurate fire from our 8.8cm self-propelled guns destroyed enemy gun positions which allowed our troops to capture Narol.

His lecture contains a number of interesting tactical lessons. Specialized units, in this case PzAbwAbt 8, must always be prepared to perform duties beyond that of a tank destroyer unit.

As a tank destroyer battalion, PzAbwAbt 8 was uniquely equipped with two companies armed with the ubiquitous 3.7cm PaK, and ten heavy-hitting *Schartenbrecher*. Additionally the 4.Kp was armed with the 2cm FlaK 38 which provided not only anti-aircraft protection, but was also deadly when used against ground targets, light armour and vehicles.

The first reports of combat involving self-propelled guns confirmed the aspirations and expectations of the military planners.

The true cross-country mobility of the *Schartenbrecher* in all conditions had yet to be proven, but when compared to the towed gun it was much quicker to bring into action against an enemy target.

For those who had favoured the SP gun and promoted the formation of fighting units, this was a true vindication. Now military planners were faced with the task of finding sufficient funds to produce the required number of vehicles.

A 10.5cm leFH 18 being loaded on a Mercedes-Benz L3000 3-ton truck; the gun weighed some 1,985kg it was easily transportable this way.

5

FRANCE AND THE BALKANS

After German forces had completed the occupation of Denmark and Norway, Hitler turned his attention to the west and initiated *Fall Gelb* (Plan Yellow), the invasion of the Low Countries and his ultimate goal; France.

Bunkerflak in Combat

The I./s PzJgAbt 8 had marched into the Low Countries and then entered France to support 1.PzDiv and 2.PzDiv commanded by Heinz Guderian.

After the conclusion of *Fall Gelb*, a questionnaire was sent to all Panzer divisions involved in the invasion. All units unilaterally confirmed that the 8.8cm FlaK gun had proved deadly for taking out bunkers and defeating heavy tanks, and again many requested that the gun be mounted in a *Sturmgeschütz* as a heavy tank destroyer for the infantry divisions (see extract from the *Waffenamt* pamphlet below).

In August 1940, an evaluation was undertaken of how successful the Panzer divisions had been in combat, in particular the flexible deployment of improvised *Kampfgruppen* (battle groups):

Report on Kampfgruppen

The Panzer division is divided into a tank and rifle brigade and this combination has proven practical and suited to the type of combat experienced in the west.

Allotment of support weapons required by both tank and rifle brigade:

- PzBrig with 8.8cm FlaK-Battery
- A light FlaK-Battery (self-propelled)
- Panzer Pioneer Company (armoured engineers)
- An Artillery Battalion (leFH)

After the fall of France, sIG Kp (Sfl) 703 was returned to its garrison. A 15cm sIG 33 auf PzKpfw I from the unit, which has been decorated with flowers for a victory parade, carries some spare running wheels on the glacis plate, a lesson learned in the first days of combat.

The 10.5cm leFH 18 auf Gw IVb was the first true self-propelled artillery gun which had the gun mounted in a rotatable turret. The side and front plating of the open-topped turret only provided the crew with protection against shrapnel and infantry fire: A shell bursting overhead could be fatal to the crew. Only ten of the type were built.

This grouping of equipment has proven to meet most situations. The 8.8cm FlaK, protected by our tanks, were used to combat heavy enemy tanks. Ideally these batteries would be mounted on SP carriages. On a number of occasions the towed FlaK batteries were positioned on higher ground to guard our battlefront.

The light FlaK batteries, mounted on half-track vehicles [SdKfz 10/4], provided excellent anti-aircraft protection; on several occasions these were used in the anti-tank role and were more successful than our PzKpfw II.

The panzer pioneer company, as long as it operates under the cover of our armour, has proved to be very efficient at clearing such items as road blocks and barbed-wire obstacles.

The escorting light artillery can, like the 8.8cm FlaK, be highly effective but only if it is protected by our armour.

In conclusion, the value of mobility and armour protection was fully recognized even for support services and weapons.

15cm sIG 33 auf PzKpfw I Ausf B

In 1938, Altmärkische Kettenwerke (Alkett) completed 38 of the type by utilizing the overhauled hull and running gear of a PzKpfw I Ausf B.

Six companies were established and each was supplied with six guns:

sIG Kp (Sfl) 701 issued to 9.PzDiv
sIG Kp (Sfl) 702 issued to 1.PzDiv

sIG Kp (Sfl) 703 issued to 2.PzDiv
sIG Kp (Sfl) 704 issued to 5.PzDiv
sIG Kp (Sfl) 705 issued to 7.PzDiv
sIG Kp (Sfl) 706 issued to 10.PzDiv

15cm sIG 33 auf PzKpfw I Ausf B

Calibre	15cm
Ammunition stowage	n/a
Gun barrel (service life)	6,000 rounds
Combat weight	8,636kg
Engine power	100hp
Speed (maximum)	35kph
Range (road/cross country)	n/a
Crew	Four
Radio equipment	None
Production	38 (on PzKpfw I)

The *Sturmgeschütz* (StuG – assault gun) was introduced as a support weapon to equip infantry divisions; an ambitious goal that was never achieved. Instead the divisions were equipped with self-propelled infantry guns.

The 8.8cm FlaK auf ZgKw 12t (SdKfz 8) *Bunkerknacker* was by any standards an enormous vehicle, and originally designed to destroy any enemy fortifications which stood in the way of the German advance. The 8.8cm *Flugabwehrkanone* (FlaK — anti-aircraft gun) 18 was deadly accurate and very effective; it was also used with much success against enemy heavy armour.

On 6 June 1940, the department of the *General der Infantrie* submitted a report based on the experiences of sIG Kompanie 706 (Sfl) to the *Oberbefehlshaber des Heeres* (commander-in-chief of the army):

Attached is a preliminary experience report on the sIG company during its deployment from 10 May to 4 June 1940:

I. General

1) The sIG 33 auf PzKpfw I Ausf B in its present form has not performed well. However the gun, if it could be used in action, was very effective and fully met our expectations.

2) The PzKpfw I chassis proved to be too weak. The running gear, although overhauled at Alkett, was still considerably worn after many years in service. Most failures (up to 60 percent) occurred with the clutches, the brakes and the tracks.

3) Most sIG companies could not keep pace with the marching speed of the tank division, which often exceeded 30kph. For this reason we advise to attach the sIG companies to infantry divisions for the coming combat.

II. Organization

1) The number of officers in the company is too low. When attached in platoon strength to the rifle companies, our NCOs could not give orders. Thus platoon leaders must be officers.

2) The *Richtkreis-Unteroffizier* II (instrument NCO in charge of the aiming circle) in the platoon is redundant as is the leader of the ammunition squad; this can be managed by the *Feuerwerker* (ordnance technical sergeant). But two mechanics must be added the personnel of the workshop company.

3) It is essential that another heavy truck is issued to transport sufficient spare parts, especially tracks, brake and clutch linings, and final-drive sprockets.

Two of the three radio cars and crews in the company can be withdrawn.

III. Combat

1) The commitment complied with regulations published in the respective pamphlets. The companies were attached to rifle brigades with single platoons attached to the rifle regiments of battalions. Combat usually involved a single sIG 33 gun firing from a concealed position at ranges varying from 50 to 4,000m. But, the front gun shield was repeatedly penetrated by armour-piercing infantry ammunition.

Not surprisingly, these remarks reveal a number of problems with the basic vehicles, many of which were predictable as only the chassis from older PzKpfw I were used for the conversion.

After the surrender of France, 10.PzDiv answered the standardized questionnaire sent to all combat units involved:

Question: Did the organization of the *Schützenbrigade* (rifle brigade) meet the expectations?

Answer: With regard to the organization of a *Schützenbrigade* with two rifle regiments, each having two rifle battalions and one sIG company. The division suggests providing all rifle battalions and infantry gun companies with self-propelled guns organized in the same way as a sIG company, which was attached to the division at beginning of the campaign.

In a combat situation, the gun crew was extremely vulnerable to enemy fire due to the open superstructure of a *Bunkerknacker*. Before advancing towards an enemy pill box or other concrete fortification they would have be assured that the area had been cleared of enemy forces. When deployed for defence against enemy armour the vehicle would fire from a concealed position.

Two 8.8cm FlaK (Sfl), built on the SdKfz 8 chassis, *Bunkerknacker* vehicles during the rapid advance by German forces through the Ardennes in June 1940. A lone French officer has been captured and awaits interrogation.

However, experiences noted by this company, have shown that the PzKpfw I tank chassis did not, in any way, meet expectations. The sIG gun is too heavy for this chassis. Often when advancing, the company could not keep pace with the division. If it remains impossible to find a suitable chassis, we suggest that these guns are loaded on flatbed trailers and towed by prime movers. The division gained much experience after operating with the PzAbt 66 during the Polish campaign, which used flatbed trailers to a great extent. However, the division once again requests that the present chassis of the sIG (Sf) be significantly improved.

At the time of the invasion of France, German military planners simply did not have sufficient funding or access to the latest armoured vehicle chassis on which to develop new types of self-propelled artillery. In this context the sIG 33 auf PzKpfw I Ausf B must be considered as a simple temporary solution driven by the lack of mobile artillery.

Three units, 8.PzDiv, 9.PzDiv and 10.PzDiv ventured even further with their demands, urging a reorganization of a divisional artillery regiment:

- One battalion leFH 18 (Sfl), with a range of 8,000m
- One battalion leFH 18 motorized traction (Zgkw)
- One mixed heavy battalion (sFH 18 or s K 18), motorized traction (Zgkw)

The Krupp-designed PzSfl IVb was an uncomplicated and compact design which utilized a shortened Panzer IV hull. The type mounted a modified 10.5cm leFH 18 which had a similar performance to a 10.5cm *Sturmhaubitze* (StuH - assault howitzer) 42.

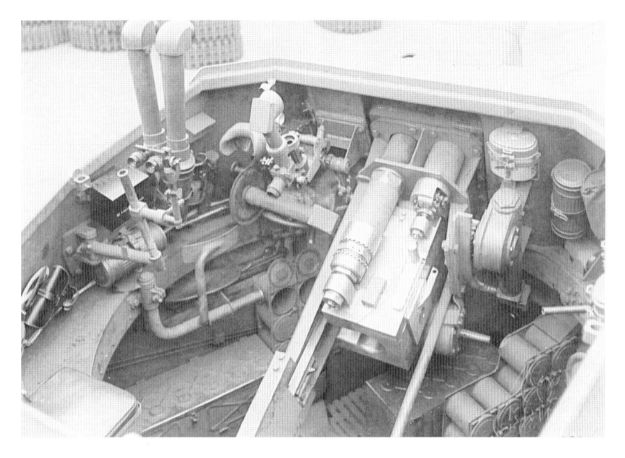

Above: The interior of the turret on a PzSfl IVb was somewhat cramped. The seats for the gun commander and the gunner could be folded away when in action. Note the *Scherenfernrohr* (scissor-type periscope) and also the *Zielfernrohr* (gun sight) ZF (Sfl) 2a.

Left: A FuSprechGer 'a' radio, for the commander, was installed in the the rear of the turret. A loudspeaker was also fitted to allow the crew to follow the action during a mission. An official Krupp document states that total of 60 shells with charges could be stowed inside the vehicle.

The 15cm sIG 33 auf PzKpfw I was a basic design. After removing the turret and tank superstructure the complete gun, including wheels, was mounted on the hull. A compartment to protect the gun and crew was fabricated from thin armour. The conversion added some 2,800kg to the original 6,000kg weight of the PzKpfw I.

The batteries, three in each battalion, were to have four guns each in accordance with organizational structures. Also it was considered necessary to appoint a highly experienced artillery commander, since reinforcing units would be frequently attached to the division. A small reconnaissance/observation battalion completed their demands.

It is evident that their main concern remained the lack of mobility and not firepower; the only gun requested was the 10.5cm leFH 18.

During establishment of the *Wehrmacht*, the *Waffenamt* maintained and updated their own lists of all weapons and vehicles currently under development.

Included in the lists were details for six types of self-propelled gun. At that time the term *Panzer-Selbstfahrlafette* (PzSfl – armoured self-propelled tank gun) began to be used and later changed to *Panzerhaubitze* (tank howitzer).

It is important to note that some of the projects would be deployed at *Heeresgruppen* (army group) level and were therefore available for all units, even infantry divisions.

Schwere Betonknacker (Heavy Concrete Buster)

In the years leading up to the war, military planners in Germany gave great importance to attacking and defeating the heavy fortifications built at strategic points on the borders of Czechoslovakia, Belgium and France and initiated the

Above: The tracks were very prone to damage, and breakages were a frequent problem. The crew of 'Douaumont' has fitted spare track links below the superstructure, adding even more weight to an already overloaded chassis.

Left: Although it appeared to have strength, surprisingly the superstructure was fabricated from 10mm-thick mild-steel plating and was not proof against infantry armour-piercing bullets.

development of weapons suitable for the task. The pamphlet published by the *Waffenamt* shows that two of these weapons were self-propelled guns: a 10cm K L/52 for delivery in summer of 1942 and a heavier 12.8cm K L/62 for the summer of 1943. Unusually for the German armaments industry, development proceeded faster than predicted and both types were ready for service 12 months early. It was planned to produce both types in large numbers. (See Table 5.1)

15cm sIG 33 for Short and Medium-range Missions

It was planned to develop a self-propelled chassis for the standard 15cm sIG 33 to equip the motorized rifle regiments in a tank division. The *Waffenamt* document demanded that a tank chassis capable of travelling at high speed be used. Another requirement seen as essential was that the gun should be able to be quickly dismounted.

These requirements were not achievable in the short term which resulted in the rushed production of the 15cm sIG 33 auf Fahrgestell PzKpw I Ausf B for the invasion of the Low Countries and France.

But the type did not meet one of the main features; the option to dismount the gun from the chassis. Although this was to remain an essential requirement for German military planners it was never realized.

The ability to dismount the gun from the vehicle had a number of advantages, but also a number of drawbacks. Most importantly, a specialized fully tracked

Schwerer Betonknacker

Situation January 1940

Type/ Designation	Intended Purpose	Weapon	Armour Protection	Weight	Crew	Speed (max)	Drawings Available	Anticipated Start of Production	Remarks
Originally Stated Target									
Schwerer Betonknacker (PzSfl)	Combat of heavily armoured fortifications	a) 10cm K L/62	Front: 50mm Side: 20–30mm	22t	Five	40kph			Basing on medium tank chassis
		b) 12.8cm K L/81	Front: 50mm Side: 20–30mm	30t	Five	25kph			Basing on heavy tank chassis
Realistically First Attainable Objective									
Schwerer Betonknacker (PzSfl)	as above	a) 10cm K L/62	Front: 50mm Side: 20–30mm	22t	Five	25kph	1 March 1941	Autumn 1942	as above
		b) 12.8cm K L/81	Front: 50mm Side: 20–30mm	30t	Five	25kph	1 October 1941	Summer 1943	as above

Schweres Infanteriegeschütz

Situation January 1940

Type/ Designation	Intended Purpose	Weapon	Armour Protection	Weight	Crew	Speed (max)	Drawings Available	Anticipated Start of Production	Remarks
Originally Stated Target									
Schweres Infanteriegeschütz (PzSfl)	Combat of living targets behind and under cover	15cm sIG 33	Front: 50mm Side: 20mm	12t	Four	67kph			Rapid dismounting of the gun, motorized transport of the gun over longer distances
Realistically First Attainable Objective									
Schweres Infanteriegeschütz (PzSfl)	As intended stated target, but with restrictions	a) The demand for quick dismounting is yet to be fulfilled b) Side armour is only proof against 7.92mm armour-piercing bullets				40kph	1 April 1941	Autumn 1942	
Current Solution									
15cm sIG 33 auf Fahrgestell PzKpfw I Ausf B	sIG 33 self-propelled gun	15cm sIG 33	Proof against 7.92mm armour-piercing bullets	7t	Three	40kph	Ready	No longer in production	

Leichte Feldhaubitze

Situation
January 1940

Type/Designation	Intended Purpose	Weapon	Armour Protection	Weight	Crew	Speed (max)	Drawings Available	Anticipated Start of Production	Remarks
Originally Stated Target									
Leichte Feldhaubitze (PzSfl)	Armoured howitzer for tank units	10.5cm le FH 18	Front: 20mm Side: 7.92mm armour-piercing bullets	17 t	Four	60kph		Winter 1942/43	Built on the chassis of a medium tank
Realistically First Attainable Objective									
Leichte Feldhaubitze (PzSfl)	As intended stated target								

artillery force would always be capable of keeping pace with advancing tanks and be ready to provide instant supporting fire.

To dismount the guns and establish a line of fixed positions was alien to Guderian and his prosecution of a mobile war. As the war progressed more ideas for a dismounting a gun were trialled, but many were too complex to produce and would have consumed valuable resources and production time. (See lower table on page 95)

10.5cm leFH 18/1 for Medium and Long-range Artillery Missions

The design and development of the *Panzerhaubitze*, a fast-moving self-propelled gun capable of keeping pace with an advancing Panzer division, was initiated in early 1940.

The 10.5cm leFH 18, was the standard light field howitzer for an artillery regiment in a Panzer division, but a modified version was to be mounted on the first true *Panzerhaubitze*. A special chassis was designed which utilized a number of components from the PzKpfw IV. However, the new chassis was shortened and fitted with six running wheels, allowing a reduction in vehicle weight. The gun, designated 10.5cm leFH 18/1, was mounted in the centre of the chassis and protected by an open turret which could be traversed 35° to each side. The gun barrel could be elevated from -10° to +40°, approximately the same as the towed version.

By 1940, no substantial plans had been be drawn up to mount a 15cm sFH 18, the heavy weapon of the artillery regiments in a Panzer division, on a self-propelled chassis. (See table opposite)

10.5cm leFH18/1 auf Gw IVb (Sfl)

Calibre	10.5cm
Ammunition stowage	60 rounds
Gun barrel (service life)	6,000 rounds
Firing height	1,840mm
Combat weight	18,289kg
Engine power	188hp
Speed (maximum)	35kph
Range (road/cross country)	240/130km
Crew	Four
Radio equipment	FuSprGer 'a'
Production	10

Left: A 15cm sIG 33 auf PzKpfw I from sIG Kp (Sfl) 705 with elements of 7.PzDiv, including PzKfw 38(t) and PzKpfw II tanks, during the invasion of France. The close cooperation between tanks, the rifle regiment and attached self-propelled gun company proved to be very effective.

Sturmgeschütz

Situation January 1940

Type/ Designation	Intended Purpose	Weapon	Armour Protection	Weight	Crew	Speed (max)	Drawings Available	Anticipated Start of Production	Remarks
Originally Stated Target									
Sturmgeschütz (PzSfl)	Not specified								
Realistically First Attainable Objective									
Sturmgeschütz (PzSfl) (lange 7.5 cm Kanone)	Heavily armoured escort gun for the infantry	7.5cm L/41	Front: 50mm Side: 30mm	21t	Four	40kph	1 March 1941	Spring 1942	On PzKpfw III chassis
Current Solution									
Sturmgeschütz (PzSfl)	Heavily armoured escort gun for the infantry	7.5cm L/24	Front: 50mm Side: 30mm	20.2t	Four	40kph	Ready	In full production	On PzKpfw III chassis

8.8cm Flak L/56

Situation January 1940

Type/ Designation	Intended Purpose	Weapon	Armour Protection	Weight	Crew	Speed (max)	Drawings Available	Anticipated Start of Production	Remarks
Originally Stated Target									
Schwerer Panzerjäger (PzSfl)	Heavy tank hunter, at the same time assault gun and light concrete buster	8.8cm L/56	Front: 50mm Side: 20–30mm	22t	Four	50kph	1 January 1942	Autumn 1942	To be built on a medium tank chassis
Realistically First Attainable Obective									

As stated above in Autumn 1942

Sturmgeschütz

Originally it was planned to deploy a StuG battalion equipped with 18 guns in each infantry division. Unsurprisingly this could not be achieved, and the units were issued at army group level instead of being allocated to various units on special order.

The *Waffenamt* document would imply that the gun originally specified for the StuG was the Krupp-built 7.5cm *Kanone* L/41, a long-barrelled assault gun that could be used as a tank destroyer or even as a light *Betonknacker.* However, this would thwart all hitherto research. Instead, a 7.5cm KwK L/24 gun was mounted as a temporary solution in clear contradiction to ordnance policy – perhaps caused by a misunderstanding between staff members at the *Waffenamt.*

For the highly successful StuG, more powerful long-barrel guns with improved armour penetration were introduced in spring 1942. A 7.5cm StuK L/43, manufactured by Rheinmetall, was eventually mounted. (See Table 5.4)

Schwerer Panzerjäger

The proposal for a *schwerer Panzerjäger* (heavy tank destroyer) emerged in 1940. The excellent penetration data of the 8.8cm FlaK seemed to suggest that it would be the ideal gun to use as a self-propelled multi-purpose artillery piece.

Although this ambitious project did not progress beyond a proposal, *Sturmgeschütz* units equipped with the 7.5cm StuK L/24 gun were quick to demand the soonest possible delivery of what they viewed as a superior vehicle. (See Table 5.5)

In October 1940, the *Waffenkommission der Artillerie* (weapon commission of the artillery) began to make suggestions for the type of weapons that would equip a future peacetime army. This appears to be somewhat cynical, since Hitler had already decided to carry his war into Russia.

However, the report states that there were 40 different guns with 13 separate calibres in service with the German artillery, and more than 90 shell types and 140 different types of fuse. It is understandable that the authorities decided to simplify this diversity. A number of changes were ordered:

- A reduction in the number of gun types.
- Develop more sophisticated [taper-bore] types to improve performance.
- Develop discarding sabot-type ammunition.
- Develop more Sonderartillerie (special artillery), including *Eisenbahngeschütz* (railway guns) and ultra-heavy calibre weapons.
- Improve the range of conventional artillery.
- Develop more self-propelled weapons.

The crew of an SdKfz 250/5 observation vehicle from a PzArtRgt wathch as a column of *Schützenpanzerwagen* (SPW – armoured personnel carriers) transports *Panzergrenadiere* to forward positions. In the background is a PzBefWg III command tank – note the *Sternantenne* (star antenna) – from the staff section of the division.

6

1941 – A TIME OF UNCERTAINTY

It was clear to German military authorities that a rapid and complete conversion of the artillery from horse-drawn and also motor vehicle towed to armoured self-propelled guns was almost impossible. However, the design and development of new types was begun, with much urgency, by the largest armaments companies.

Infantry Self-propelled Guns

The first fully tracked self-propelled gun to enter German service was the sIG 33 auf PzKpfw I.

During the Balkan campaign, three sIG (Sfl) Kp, 701, 703 and 704 were deployed. Sadly, the war diaries of 2.PzDiv, 5.PzDiv and 9.PzDiv give no further information on the assessment of these weapons. The only information available is dated 19 May 1941, when elements of 2.PzDiv – including sIG Kp (Sfl) 703 – were loaded on the transport ships *Kybfels* and *Marburg* at Patras (Peloponnese peninsula, Greece). On 21 May, they sailed for Taranto, Italy, but the captains of both vessels were unaware that HMS *Abdiel* (M39), a Royal Navy minelayer, had sown a field of 150 mines between Cephalonia and Levkas during the hours of darkness. At 14:00hrs, some 11 miles east of Cape Dukato, *Kybfels* struck a mine and sank very quickly; a short time later *Marburg* fell to the same fate, but caught fire and burned for several hours before sinking. A total of 226 personnel were lost, along with the valuable cargo of vehicles and equipment.

A 15cm sIG 33 (horse drawn) at full recoil as it is fired at a distant target: The heavy infantry gun had excellent destructive firepower at ranges up to 4,780m.

A column of 15cm sIG 33 auf PzKpfw I driving along a Russian road: The hard surface was a rarity, as most were rutted tracks which became almost impassible during the *Rasputitsa* (mud season. During long-distance marches, the overweight vehicle suffered many failures with the running gear, which was never modified or improved.

It is thought that the tanks and other heavy equipment from 2.PzDiv had been dispatched by ship to Taranto a few days earlier. However, it is noted in a report, dated later in May 1942, that sIG Kp 703 had been reformed.

During *Unternehmen* (operation) Barbarossa, 1.PzDiv, 2.PzDiv, 5.PzDiv, 7.PzDiv, 9.PzDiv and 10.PzDiv retained their sIG (Sfl) attachments.

On 18 September 1941, sIG 33 Kp 702 (1.PzDiv) submitted an after-action report, which is in some respect surprising:

sIG Kp 702 (mot S)   Company command post

Experience report sIG (mot S)
(Older version with PzKpfw I Ausf B chassis)

Despite being thoroughly aware of the shortcomings of the type, the sIG (mot S) has performed very well as an assault gun during the campaign in Russia. This is in contrast to the first combat deployment in France, when the unit was afflicted by a number of serious problems. However our troops have benefited from the long training phase and become accustomed to all mechanical vagaries and adept at correcting any faults.

The sIG (mot S) is the ideal assault gun for the lead echelon of a *Kampfgruppe* in the Panzer division.

The low trajectory of the gun, when firing with a No.4 charge, is very effective for attacking a point target such as a bunker or dug-in artillery, or machine-gun nests and mortar positions, with a minimal expenditure of ammunition. Due to having a fully tracked chassis the vehicle can be moved quickly to attack a fresh target. Also by being armoured, the sIG (mot S) can also be deployed in an open position, and this can have a demoralizing effect on enemy forces; many cease firing and give away away their positions. The gun is not suitable for use as an anti-tank gun, but it must be emphasized that in an emergency situation it can be used to attack enemy armour. Just the massive effect of a 15cm high-explosive shells detonating near enemy tanks will normally cause the attack to turn away; this was even applicable to the 52t heavy tank [Soviet KV]. A stationary tank or any that approaches head-on can be destroyed at 300 to 400m range by firing two or three shells propelled by the No.4 charge.

In most instances a combat company was supported by a single self-propelled gun, but any action involving the platoon would be the exception: the guns would be concealed in a covered position: Some 80 percent of all rounds were fired from an open position.

The range of the portable radio sets supplied to a company, the Torn FuSprechGer 'a' [fire control] and the TornFuGer 'g' [command], is far too low. It is most important to replace these with more powerful equipment.

The workshop facilities for the company must be improved and enlarged. The lack of an 8-ton *Zugmaschine* [SdKfz 7] and a flatbed trailer, to enable the recovery of damaged guns

Workshop engineers have erected a simple gantry, assembled from heavy timbers, to remove the superstructure and gun from the PzKpfw I chassis. Note a pintle to secure the gun carriage is mounted on the rear.

The crew of this 15cm sIG 33 auf PzKpfw I, of sIG Kp (Sfl) 702 in 2.PzDiv, has applied a coating of whitewash paint to their vehicle in an attempt to camouflage it for winter conditions in Russia.

for repair, is a very serious problem. Recovery services at divisional level were insufficient and extremely slow at recovering any damaged gun. This was observed when two were lost during the advance and despite of their exact positions being reported (as required in regulations) neither vehicle was recovered immediately. However, both were later recovered by crews from the Speer organization, but were not returned to the company. If a tractor and flatbed trailer had been available, these precious guns would have been returned directly to our workshop unit for repair and be available for service after seven days.

The resupply to our guns worked satisfactorily, this was due to the dedication to his task by the leader of the ammunition squad. However, it has become obvious that the standard Opel *Blitz* truck has poor cross-country mobility and a lack of cargo capacity. Since a large stock of ammunition cannot be carried on the gun, the resupply team has to follow in close proximity. As a consequence, the delivery of heavy cross-country trucks must be considered a vital necessity.

Conclusion
A mechanically improved sIG (mot S), now equipped with the required radio equipment, is a match for most modern weaponry. These self-propelled guns will prove indispensable for combat in rugged terrain, over marshland or through wooded areas. A rapid advance is possible when travelling over hard-packed tracks or paved roadways.

Performance report submitted after the deployment near St Petersburg:

1. Ammunition consumption: 1,640 15cm shells
2. Destroyed targets:
   a) 24 bunkers
   b) 13 anti-tank guns
   c) 31 guns
   d) Six tanks

3. Casualties:
Killed: Two NCOs, 11 enlisted men
Wounded: 11 NCOs, 39 enlisted men

4. Technical report:
During the days of marching, combat and rest, the following repairs were undertaken.

Replaced items:
1,057 track bolts
392 track links
68 running wheels

A 15cm sIG 33 auf PzKpfw I, of sIG Kp 702 is parked on a fascine of small tree trunks to prevent it sinking in the mud as the snow thaws. The stack of ammunition in wicker baskets behind the vehicle indicates that the gun is ready for a fire-support mission.

This 15cm sIG 33 auf PzKpfw I has been hit in the engine compartment and the explosion has torn apart the superstructure. The high temperatures generated in the resulting fire, have melted the alloy parts of the wheels, leaving only white powder.

Eight idler wheels

Two drive sprockets

Eight sprocket rings

28 bogeys

Two final drives

Five return rollers

Nine leaf springs

Two shock absorbers

12 brake pads

Two clutches

Not covered is the repair work carried out in the workshop which included the complete overhaul or the installation of a new Maybach engine.

[Note: In many wartime documents, the sIG auf PzKpfw I is identified with the suffix 'Sf' or 'Sfl' – *Selbstfahrlafette* (self-propelled chassis), but 'PzSfl' was also used to indicate that the vehicle was armoured. However, this report uses the suffix 'mot S'; 'mot' would normally refer to 'motorized', but the reason for the 'S' remains a mystery.]

The statement from Kp 702 is clearly contradictory in many areas. Operational experience in France had shown that the gun was too heavy for the PzKpfw I chassis. A *Rüststand* report published by the *Waffenamt* in June 1940, was annotated with this handwritten comment:

'Chassis far too light and not suitable for the 15cm sIG 33'

On the other hand it seems that the unit had become fully acquainted with the peculiarities of the type, especially the drivers who knew the capabilities of their vehicles.

The destructive power of the 15cm sIG 33 on a target had been witnessed by many units on the battlefield. Now, mounted on a full-tracked chassis it had become a formidable weapon able to attack an increasing range of targets. It was possible to quickly follow the infantry, firing accurately at close range on identified targets with devastating effect. Many Russian tanks were observed turning away when being engaged by what they assumed to be a superior opponent, the same action was also observed often during the first months of *Unternehmen* Barbarossa. However, there were some mitigating circumstances; Soviet tank commanders and crews were poorly trained, their tanks lacked adequate observation means and they did not have radio equipment.

In 1942, sIG Kp 707 was transferred to North Africa to fight with 90.LeDiv. As part of their pre-combat preparation, the crew is using a *Rohrwischer* (barrel brush) to clean the internal surface of the 15cm gun barrel.

During action in North Africa a 15cm sIG 33 auf PzKpfw II suffered a catastrophic mechanical failure. German field engineers made the decision to mount, with much success, the valuable gun on a redundant PzKpfw III hull.

Also until the T-34 arrived on the battlefront, Soviet tanks were poorly armed and had inadequate armour protection.

The decision the commander of sIG Kp 702 made to deploy the sIG 33 auf PzKpfw I (Sfl) in the role of a *Sturmgeschütz* (StuG – assault gun) ignored a significant weakness. The type was vulnerable in the face of dogged resistance from well-led enemy troops, as a hit from an anti-tank rifle would penetrate the thin armour. Even armour-piercing infantry fire could pierce the gun shield.

It was impossible for the simple self-propelled gun to fulfill the role of a *Sturmgeschütz*. Later in 1942, the *Waffenamt* issued clear restrictions on the deployment of what they describe as *Waffenträger* (weapon carrier) for any dangerous missions.

The report concludes with the suggestion for the development of a 15cm sIG 33 gun mounted on a new self-propelled chassis with better cross-country mobility.

In May 1942, *Heeresgruppe Mitte* (army group centre) reported that the attached sIG companies would not be replenished due to the low number of self-propelled guns (on the PzKpfw I Ausf B hull) being available. All redundant personnel were transferred to the infantry school at Döberitz to assist in the establishment of new companies, which were to be issued with the new *schweres Infanteriegeschütz 33/1 auf Geschützwagen 38(t)* (sIG auf Gw – heavy

A 15cm sIG 33 auf PzKpfw II traverses the undulating sand and scrub terrain of North Africa. The deployment of the type was a complete disaster as the PzKpfw II chassis and running gear was overloaded, and the type was seriously underpowered.

infantry gun on weapon carrier) built on a PzKpfw 38(t) chassis. Training was set to begin in October 1942, but this date could not be kept.

15cm sIG 33 auf PzKpfw II

In May 1941, a new entry in the *Rüststand* showed a new type designated the sIG 33 B (Sfl) and although the base chassis for the vehicle is not mentioned it was indeed that of a PzKpfw II: a logical step in an attempt to eliminate the many flaws of the PzKpfw I. By mid-1940 Alkett had completed a *Versuchsstück* (prototype) which, unsuccessfully, mounted a sIG 33 (without the wheeled carriage) on a basically unchanged PzKpfw II hull. It was noted during firing trials at Kummersdorf, that the hull was stable under the heavy recoil of the gun; it was also noted that there was a serious lack of room inside the vehicle.

After assessing the report, Alkett decided to develop a new hull which was widened and lengthened, requiring a sixth road wheel to be fitted.

The result was the O-series and Alkett was contracted to produce 12 units which had to be delivered by 15 September 1941. However, in late September the *Waffenamt* wrote requesting a firm delivery date. In January 1942, the first seven sIG 33 auf PzKpfw II entered service and the final five were delivered in February 1942.

15cm sIG 33 auf PzKpfw II	
Calibre	15cm
Ammunition stowage	10 rounds
Gun barrel (service life)	6,000 rounds
Firing height	n/a
Combat weight	12t
Speed (maximum)	45kph
Range (maximum)	100km
Crew	Four
Communication	FuSprechGer 'f'
Production	12 (0-series)

The 12 guns were issued to two independent companies, sIG 33 Kp (mot S) 707 and 708, which had been established in September 1941. The companies were then sent to North Africa, where they were attached to 90.leDiv.

An after-action report published in *Rommel's Funnies*, T. Jentz (Darlington Productions) confirms that during the first transfer marches a large number of these guns failed due to mechanical problems. The report concludes by noting that the vehicles were unsuitable for combat in North Africa, mainly due to a number of mechanical problems. However, the destructive power of the 15cm sIG 33 was still regarded as being highly effective. A report published in December 1942 notes that all 12 of the sIG 33 auf PzKpfw II had been lost.

A *Waffenamt* had noted in a *Rüststand* dated July 1942, that no further 15cm sIG were to be built and that the type would not go into mass production as a new type using a PzKpfw 38(t) chassis was to be developed.

Heavy Flat-Trajectory Guns
10cm K 18 auf PzSfl IVa

At the beginning of *Unternehmen* Barbarossa the two s 10cm K 18 auf PzSfl IVa, developed and produced by Krupp, were ready for combat and both were issued to PzJgAbt 521 (Sfl), an independent unit deployed at *Heerestruppen* (army troop) level.

Although designed as a *Bunkerknacker* (bunker buster) they were often used in the anti-tank role. However, the standard Panzergranate armour-piercing round lacked accuracy and power, but as a consequence the precious experience gained in battle led to the development of more advanced types of self-propelled gun for both artillery and tank destroyer forces.

Right: In March 1942, sIG (Sfl) Kp 707, equipped with seven 15cm sIG 33 auf PzKpfw II, was ordered to the port of Naples where the unit was to embark on a transport ship for the voyage to Tripoli and action in North Africa.

During operations in
North Africa in 1942, the
engine of this 15cm sIG 33
auf PzKpfw II overheated
and caught fire, which
spread to the fuel tanks
and ammunition, which
exploded, destroying the
vehicle.

12.8cm K 40 auf PzSfl V

In 1939, Henschel had been contracted to design and develop a weapon carrier for a heavy field gun derived from the new 12.8cm FlaK 40. Two prototypes were built using the chassis and components from the VK 30.01; one of the prototypes for the PzKpfw VI Tiger heavy tank.

In early 1942, both had been tested and accepted for service. Together with the sole remaining PzSfl IVa they were combined to form a *Panzerjäger* platoon attached to PzJgAbt (Sfl) 521.

Due to the design of both the PzSfl IVa and PzSfl V types, their 10cm and 12.8cm guns could only be used for flat-trajectory fire against a target. Also as part of a tank destroyer battalion the types would be used to attack Soviet armour. More detail of their commitment can be found in: *Panzerjäger Volume 1* (Osprey 2018).

Despite numerous shortcomings with the design and mechanical problems, these early self-propelled guns did provide military planners and engineers with the valuable experience to design new types in the future.

In 1941, two s 10cm auf PzKpfw IV (PzSfl IVa) were built and served on the Eastern Front for *Unternehmen* (Operation) Barbarossa. In the initial stages of the invasion one was lost due to the engine overheating which caused the ammunition to ignite; the resulting explosion ripped the vehicle to pieces.

A 15cm sIG 33 auf PzKpfw I carries the tactical markings for sIG Kp 704 and the emblem of 5.PzDiv.

12.8cm K 40 auf PzSfl V

Calibre	12.8cm
Ammunition stowage	15 rounds
Gun barrel (service life)	n/a
Combat weight	37,086kg
Speed (maximum)	25kph
Range (maximum)	170km
Crew	Five
Communication	FuSprGer 'f'
Production	Two prototypes

After the fall of France, Alfred Becker began work to modify 12 abandoned British-built Vickers Light Tank Mk VI to mount a 10.5cm leFH 16 from his artillery unit. The gun first saw service in World War I and was issued to horse-drawn artillery units. Becker achieved his ambition and created an effective self-propelled gun.

Captured Equipment

After the invasion of France, the battlefields were strewn with all types of abandoned military equipment including vehicles and armour. The economic situation and a constant shortage of raw materials vital to the war effort forced the Germans to make best use of this equipment. Small weapons were issued to police units or used to arm their allies and passenger cars and trucks were refurbished and issued to German military units. Much of the industrial capacity in France remained intact and many companies were ordered back into production making everything from aero engines and aircraft, to trucks for the German military.

Alfred Becker

The development of German self-propelled guns is closely connected with Alfred Becker, a very unusual man who was born in 1899 and had served as an artillery officer in World War I. At the beginning of World War II, he was conscripted and served with Artillery-Regiment 227 (227.InfDiv) and first saw action during the invasion of the Low Countries. Apparently Becker was an energetic character, who was skilled mechanic and also an adept innovator. During the advance across Holland his unit passed a column of abandoned

The engine and transmission on a Vickers Light Tank Mk VI was mounted in the front of the vehicle, making it an ideal chassis for conversion to a self-propelled gun. The superstructure, to protect the gun and crew, was fabricated from material supplied by German companies directly to Becker.

vehicles from a motorized artillery regiment. Becker, whose unit was horse drawn, decided to commandeer a number of the abandoned prime movers and began to convert his horse-drawn battery into a motorized unit: very unusual by German standards. Although details of his work remain unknown, it would be interesting to know how Becker overcame mechanical problems, and also with the supply of fuel and spare parts.

When the fighting in the west ended, 227.InfDiv was deployed near the Normandy coast as an occupation force. Here Becker began to examine the large numbers of abandoned British vehicles (including tanks) and other equipment that littered the roads. Once again he considered how to make best use of this material, presumably without being authorized by his commanders.

At first it was thought that the British-built Vickers Light Tank Mk VI was too small, but it was designed with the engine and transmission mounted in the front of the hull, making it eminently suitable for conversion to a self-propelled gun. Becker recovered a number of tanks and began to experiment on the simplest way to carry out a conversion. Firstly, he had the turret lifted off the tank and the plating over the fighting compartment removed before mounting a 10.5cm leFH 16 on the superstructure: The first firing trials were a success. Spurred by this success, Becker began ordering materials direct from Germany by using a number of his old business contacts. He used sheet steel plates to construct a small superstructure which provided some protection for the crew

During the invasion of France a large number of French-built Chenilette Lorraine 37L, a fully tracked supply vehicle, were captured. The vehicle, which usually towed a small tracked trailer, was designed to operate over rough terrain. German engineers were quick to recognize that this versatile vehicle was eminently suitable for conversion to a self-propelled SP gun.

The engine in a Lorraine 37L was mounted in the centre of the chassis, which made it more straightforward to convert and mount various types of gun, including the long-barrelled 15cm sFH 13.

and since the vehicle was light, he fabricated a small recoil spade to be fitted on the rear of the hull. Becker went on to produce twelve 10.5cm leFH 13, six lg 15cm sFH 13 self-propelled guns and a number of support vehicles including observation tanks and ammunition carriers.

During 1941, 227 InfDiv was deployed to Russia with *Heeresgruppe Nord* (army group north), which at that time was the only infantry unit issued with self-propelled artillery, and operated with much success. Quite naturally, reports of the work carried out by Becker reached officials at the *Waffenamt*, and in early 1942 he was transferred to Alkett, where he worked on the development of mobile artillery and anti-tank guns.

Return to France

Albert Speer, who became *Reichsminister für Bewaffnung und Munition* (minister of armaments and ammunitions) after the sudden death of Fritz Todt in February 1942, appointed Becker as head of a *Baukommando* (construction command) tasked with how to make best use of captured French equipment. Three factories near Paris were commandeered and put into use as workshops.

Among the many military vehicles found in France, two types of tracked support vehicle would be eminently suitable for conversion: the Renault Chenilette UE and the larger Lorraine 37L Chenilette. The UE was used as a light prime mover by tank destroyer units; the heavier Lorraine was found to be suitable for conversion to a self-propelled gun.

The Lorraine 37L was originally built as supply vehicle for the newly founded French tank divisions. The engine was mounted in the centre of the chassis of the lightly armoured vehicle which had a rear cargo bed to carry an 800kg payload. Some 432 of the type were produced and around 300 were found to be in a repairable state and were recovered and delivered to Becker. An unknown number of more seriously damaged vehicles were sent to Germany to be overhauled or scrapped.

In late 1940, an urgent call was made for more self-propelled guns to equip anti-tank and artillery units. To make up for the shortage military planners decided to make the best possible use of captured material.

The Lorraine, due to it having a centre-mounted engine, proved to be ideal. The severe economic and manufacturing situation in the Reich would certainly have influenced officials with their decision.

A number of important guns were chosen to be mounted on the Lorraine chassis:

- 7.5cm PaK 40
- Lg 15cm sFH 13
- 10.5cm leFH 18

Two batteries of self-propelled guns built using the Lorraine 37L chassis mounting a 15cm sFH 13 are lined up for inspection. By making best use of obsolete guns and ex-French army fully tracked vehicles, Alfred Becker and Alkett created a number of highly successful self-propelled guns.

Lg 15cm sFH 13 auf Lorraine

In 1941, it was decided to mount the lg 15cm sFH 13, which had entered service in 1917, on the chassis of the Lorraine 37L as a self-propelled gun. The sFH 13 was still listed in the *Rüststand* produced by the *Waffenamt*, alongside the more effective 15cm sFH 18. Some 94 from the stock of 15cm sFH 13 guns were delivered to Becker for the conversion.

Alkett was to be responsible for development and assembly, but under the direction of Becker. Without any warning, Adolf Hitler issued a directive for the immediate production of 30 vehicles for use in North Africa. The type was designated 15cm sFH 13 *auf Geschützwagen* Lorraine and Alkett successfully delivered the 30 ordered by Hitler in June 1942. The conversion was straightforward. The gun was mounted in the rear of the vehicle and the fighting compartment was fabricated from steel plates as proof against infantry armour-piercing bullets. A retractable recoil spade was fitted to the rear of the vehicle.

Initially it was intended to issue 12 of the type to 21.PzDiv, 12 to 15.PzDiv and six to 90.PzGrenDiv. Seven were lost during the voyage, so only 23 reached Benghazi [Tobruk].

The sFH 13 auf Gw Lorraine was integrated in the organizational structures of the combat units listed above, to reinforce available artillery elements.

When first delivered all 10.5cm leFH 18 auf Gw Lorraine were painted in dark grey, but in 1943 were finished in camouflage to suit the battlefront; the running gear remained painted grey.

In 1944, *Generalfeldmarschall* Rommel made an inspection of the batteries forming *gepanzerte Artillerie-Brigade* West (armoured artillery brigade west). Soon after his visit, this large formation was disbanded and all the equipment distributed to other units. Behind Rommel is a 10.5cm leFH 18/40 auf Gw H-39 (f). The annotation 'braun-arc' refers to the type of lubrication fluid for the recuperator.

Military planners, aware of the conditions in North Africa, placed restrictions on the deployment of the type and ordered that the guns be used as mobile escort artillery. The chassis proved to be mechanically reliable, but the achievable top speed was too slow to keep pace with advancing German armour. If the Lorraine became separated from the main body of the Panzer regiment it would soon be an easy target for enemy gunners. By the end of 1942, all had been lost in action.

In the meantime, *Baustab* Becker had commenced production of the type at their factories in Paris and had completed the conversion of another 64 units by August 1942.

In November 1942, the *Rüststand* stated that 19 of the guns were lost in combat and in February 1943, a further 12 were also lost. However, in May the figures were corrected and showed that 64 vehicles were available – the same number completed by *Baukommando* Becker.

15cm sFH 13 auf Gw Lorraine	
Calibre	15cm
Ammunition storage	Eight rounds
Gun barrel (service life)	n/a
Combat weight	7.5t
Speed (maximum)	35kph
Range	n/a
Crew	Four
Communication	FuSprechGer 'f'
Production	94

10.5cm leFH 18 auf Lorraine

Since the leFH 18 was the standard issue light field howitzer for all German field units it was the logical choice for it to be mounted as a self-propelled artillery gun.

The *Baukommando* Becker used the 10.5cm leFH 18 to build a further type of self-propelled gun using the Lorraine chassis. The resulting vehicle was identical to the 15cm sFH 13 auf Gw Lorraine.

According to the Rüststand statistics, 12 such vehicles were produced in November 1942. In April 1943, no 10.5cm leFH 18 auf Gw Lorraine were reported as being built. It is known that seven were lost in December 1943, but the reason and where they were deployed is unknown.

Above: In 1942, a batch of 23 lange 15cm sFH 13 auf Gw Lorraine were shipped to North Africa, to reinforce the artillery elements of several units of the *Panzerarmee Afrika* (tank army Africa). The vehicle has a recoil spade mounted on the rear and is painted in a low-contrast yellow-brown and grey-green desert camouflage scheme.

Left: A crewman standing by the side of this 10.5cm leFH 18 auf Gw Lorraine emphasizes the relatively small size of the type.

In November 1942, the first of the 12-built 10.5cm leFH auf Gw Lorraine self-propelled guns were delivered to the artillery. With some foresight, Alfred Becker decided to fit armour protection for the gun cradle and recuperator. Although frequently requested by the artillery it would not be fitted on the *Wespe* or the *Hummel*.

10.5cm leFH 18 auf Gw Lorraine

Calibre	10.5cm
Ammunition storage	30 rounds
Gun barrel (service life)	6,000 rounds
Combat weight	7.5t
Speed (maximum)	38kph
Range (road)	120km
Crew	Four
Radio equipment	FuSprechGer 'a'
Production	12

10.5cm leFH 18 auf PzKpfw B 2 (f) (PzSfl)

In March 1941, the office of the Führer ordered the production of more self-propelled guns using French tank chassis. A small series was planned using a B 2 heavy tank as the base vehicle and all the development was carried out by Rheinmetall-Borsig. In July 1942, an order was placed for 16 of the type.

The conversion was very straightforward: after removal of the gun turret a small superstructure was fabricated to protect the crew, simply mounted in place of the turret. The result was a conspicuously high vehicle which would restrict how the type could be deployed.

The vehicle would operate as escort artillery for units equipped with B2 *Flammpanzer* (flame-thrower tank).

10.5cm leFH 18/3 auf PzKpfw B 2 (f)

Calibre	10.5cm
Ammunition storage	n/a
Gun barrel (service life)	6,000 rounds
Combat weight	32.5t
Speed (maximum)	20kph
Range on road/cross country	140km/100km
Crew	Five
Radio equipment	FuSprechGer 'a'
Production	16

In late 1942, the chassis of 16 captured B1 heavy tanks were modified to mount a 10.5cm leFH 18/3. The bow-mounted 75mm gun was removed and the aperture plated over and the turret was replaced by an open-topped superstructure to protect the gun and crew. At first it was planned for the type to be deployed on the Eastern Front, but due to production delays all remained in France with the armoured artillery brigades.

In 1943, the 10.5cm leFH auf Gw B 2(f) were issued to I./PzArtRgt 93 in 26.PzDiv, where they were used on trial tactics for supporting tank formations during an advance. When 26.PzDiv was shipped to Italy, it was re-equipped with *Wespe* and *Hummel*.

10.5cm leFH 18/40 auf Gw H-39 (f) (PzSfl)

The Hotchkiss H-39 light tank was one of the most numerous French tanks for conversion at the works of *Baukommando* Becker. Although it was a compact vehicle, it proved large enough to mount a leFH 18/40 and a total of 48 were converted. Another 60 were converted to mount a 7.5cm PaK 40.

10.5cm leFH 18/40 auf Gw H-39 (f)

Calibre	10.5cm
Ammunition storage	n/a
Gun barrel – service life	6,000 rounds
Combat weight	n/a
Speed (maximum)	36kph
Range on road/cross country	150km/90km
Crew	Four
Radio equipment	FuSprechGer 'f'
Production	48

10.5cm leFH 16 auf PzKpfw FCM (f) (PzSfl)

Engineers at *Baukommando* Becker would also convert the medium tank built by Forges et Chantiers de la Méditerranée (FCM). The leFH was selected to be mounted on the chassis, but the gun was fitted with a muzzle brake to reduce recoil. A total of 48 vehicles were converted, as were another 48 mounting a 7.5cm PaK 40.

10.5cm leFH 16 auf PzKpfw FCM (f)

Calibre	10.5cm
Ammunition storage	36 rounds
Gun barrel (service life)	8,000 rounds
Combat weight	12.2t
Speed (maximum)	28kph
Range on road/cross country	200km/140km
Crew	Four
Radio equipment	FuSprechGer 'f'
Production	48

Resume

It is important to understand that the German authorities were totally aware of the shortcomings of the German war machine, and the reliance on vital resources found in occupied countries.

Thousands of soft-skinned vehicles were required and this was made obvious during the advance to Moscow. This resulted in a shortage which had to be filled with captured types, but as mentioned in many after-action reports, German troops had severe reservations as to their mechanical reliability and even cross-country mobility.

The decision to mount artillery guns on captured tank chassis was forced on the military authorities, although it must be questioned as to why they were produced in such small numbers bearing in mind the vast amount of captured material that was available. However it must have been a nightmare for the workshop services as many of the types were mechanically unreliable and the supply of spare parts somewhat erratic. Occasionally, the benefits the vehicles provided in battle outweighed the problems they caused.

Finally, the modified French vehicles did represent a great asset for the German units in France and other occupied countries where most of the self-propelled guns had been deployed.

Production figures:

- 94 – lg 15cm sFH 13 auf Gw Lorraine (f)
- 12 – 10.5cm leFH 18 auf Gw Lorraine (f)
- 48 – 10.5cm leFH 18/40 auf Gw H 39 (f)
- 48 – 10.5cm leFH 16 auf Gw FCM (f)
- 16 – 10.5cm leFH 18 auf Gw B2 (f)

To mount a 15cm sIG 33 on a PzKpfw II, the chassis had to be widened and lengthened. A total of 12 were converted and all were transported to North Africa where they were delivered to sIG Kp 707 and sIG Kp 708.

7

1942 – ADVANCED SELF-PROPELLED GUNS

The 15cm *schwere Infanteriegeschütz* (sIG – heavy infantry assault gun) 33 was the main heavy weapon of the front-line infantry. However, in 1941 the weapon was in great demand, but only 25 to 35 guns were being completed each month, which was barely enough to equip new units and replace the guns lost in combat. By August 1942 some 764 were in service.

The first self-propelled version, the 15cm sIG33 auf P3kpfwI Ausf B, had to be highly effective in countless battles, but for deployment in the new Panzer divisions it was considered too slow. In an attempt to quickly resolve this problem it was decided to mount a sIG 33 on the chassis of a PzKpfw II. A limited number of the 15cm sIG 33 auf PzKpfw II, known as the 'O' series, were built but entered service without being thoroughly tested. All were sent to North Africa, but proved to be mechanically unreliable in the hot climate, making them unsuitable for combat. As a result further production of the type was cancelled.

After the defeat of the German army at Moscow, Hitler decided to turn his attention and prepare his forces for an invasion of the Caucasus. Priority was given to the production of tanks to replenish debilitated Panzer divisions. But the situation for the Afrika Korps fighting in North Africa was becoming more desperate by the day.

15cm sIG 33/1 auf Gw 38 *Grille*

In early 1942, any disruption to tank production was out of the question, making the search for a suitable tracked chassis to carry the sIG 33 virtually impossible.

Italy 1943: A 15cm sIG 33 auf Gw 38(t) Ausf H in service with PzDiv Hermann Göring. The vehicle is from 9.Kp of the *schützen* (rifle) regiment as indicated on the clock-style insignia. The gun was supported on a rest when travelling; when the gun was brought into action this was unlocked from inside the fighting compartment and lowered. The *Grille* proved to be more robust and better suited to conditions in Italy than either the *Wespe* or *Hummel*.

A number of *Grille* self-propelled guns on the final production line at the Böhmisch-Mährische Maschinenfabrik (BMM) facility in Prague. Rivets have been used in the fabrication of the superstructure; a method preferred by BMM. The release rod for the gun traveling rest is clearly visible.

One of the tank types to be evaluated was the Czech-built PzKpfw 38(t) which was regarded as obsolete due to it having an ineffective gun and poor armour protection. However in late 1940, Alkett had already evaluated the PzKpfw 38(t) as a suitable chassis on which to mount the sIG 33 and found it was easily converted.

In April 1942, the manufacturer Böhmisch-Mährische Maschinenfabrik (BMM) was ordered to halt light tank production, and dedicate the available space to assembling self-propelled guns. The PzSfl 2, a tank destroyer armed with captured Soviet 7.62cm PaK 36(r), was the first vehicle using a PzKpfw 38(t) chassis to enter production. At that time, military planners decided to give priority to the provision of anti-tank weapons to halt the large numbers of Soviet heavy tanks appearing on the battlefront rather fulfil the requirements of the rifle regiments for an improved, effective carrier for the 15cm sIG 33.

While PzSfl 2 production continued, BMM began work on the simplest way to adapt a PzKpfw 38(t) chassis to mount a sIG 33, but design and development required some 12 months before series production could begin.

Since the PzKpfw 38(t) was a conventionally designed tank with the engine fitted in the rear, the gun had to be mounted in the centre of the hull. The PzKpfw 38(t), like many tanks manufactured in the 1930s, was fabricated from riveted armour plates; a method preferred by BMM. This made the conversion a more simple process: the turret was removed as was the roof plate over the fighting compartment. The 15cm sIG 33/1, slightly modified for the purpose, was positioned in the centre of the hull and fitted on a crucifom-shaped mounting.

A spacious angular-shaped superstructure was fitted, but this only protected the gun and crew against infantry armour-piercing ammunition and shrapnel. The type was fitted with a Fu 5 radio for battlefield communications with elements of the Panzer division.

15cm sIG 33/1 auf Gw 38(t) Ausf H

Calibre	15cm
Ammunition stowage	13 rounds
Gun barrel (life span)	6,000 rounds
Combat weight	11.5t
Performance	125hp
Speed (maximum)	42kph
Range road/cross country	185/140km
Crew	Four
Communication	Fu 5
Production	200

The prototype of the 15cm sIG 33 *Grille* Ausf H: The vehicle was very compact when compared to the earlier types built on PzKpfw I and II chassis. The type had an excellent power-to-weight ratio and weight distribution which resulted in a vehicle with superb mobility.

The new self-propelled gun was designated 15cm sIG 33/1 auf Gw 38 (SdKfz 138/1), and it became known to front-line troops as the *Grille* (cricket).

The *Grille* entered production in January/February 1943 and by June some 200 units had been accepted by the *Waffenamt* (ordnance office) for delivery to fighting units.

In May 1943 Albert Speer, the *Reichsminister* for ordnance and ammunitions, wrote to *Generalmajor* Kurt Zeitzler, *Chef Generalstab des Heeres*: (ChfGenStdH – chief of the general staff of the army).

> The production run of the sIG 33 auf PzKpfw 38(t) was initially limited to 200 units. Since the first sIG auf 38(t) issued to front-line forces operated magnificently, the Führer has ordered that any damaged PzKpfw 38(t) are to be immediately returned from the front and modified to carry the 15cm sIG 33.

It is highly possible that small numbers of the type were repaired then converted before being returned to combat units.

In the meantime BMM had totally redesigned the Gw 38 in order to improve weight distribution and to provide better access to the fighting compartment. To achieve this, the engine was moved to the centre of the hull and the gun, initially a 7.5cm PaK 40(r), was mounted at the rear, protected by a simple armoured superstructure. The type designation received the suffix Ausf K, (*motor Mitte* – centre engined).

In December 1943, due to the number of positive combat reports being received, it was decided to increase production of the type.

Large numbers of SdKfz 253 observation vehicles, originally designed for use by the *Sturmartillerie* (assault artillery) were also issued to Panzer divisions. A *Scherenfernrohr* (scissors-type periscope) has been fitted on a tripod and mounted on an SdKfz 235 from 19.PzDiv; note the periscope has been fitted with lens hoods to reduce glare.

A *Grille* Ausf H of 26.PzDiv: the divisional and tactical markings have been stencilled on the superstructure. The identifier 'I 12' indicates that it is in service with one of the two rifle regiments in the division. The vehicle would have been delivered painted dark, but the crew has camouflaged it by applying small patches and stripes of dark brown and olive green.

To distinguish between the two versions, the designation of the first production batch received the suffix Ausf H (*motor Hinten* – rear engined). An unarmed version was being built at the same time to serve as a *Munitions-Fahrzeug* (ammunition carrier). Interestingly, the type could be fitted with a gun by field engineers to replace a *Grille* that had been damaged or destroyed in battle, to maintain the combat strength of a company.

According to *Rüststand* statistical data, some 180 *Grille* Ausf K vehicles were produced, with another 102 built as *Munitions-Fahrzeuge*.

15cm sIG 33/2 auf Gw 38(t) Ausf K

Calibre	15cm
Ammunition storage	15 rounds
Gun barrel (life span)	6,000 rounds
Combat weight	11.5t
Performance	150hp
Speed (maximum)	42kph
Range (road/cross country	180/140km
Crew	Four
Communication	Fu 5
Production	180

A *Grille* Ausf H being carefully manoeuvred on to a snow-covered railway wagon. Whenever possible the German army relied on rail transport not only for speed, but also to avoid the mechanical damage experienced on long marches.

The *Rüststand* also noted that combat losses were surprisingly low, and in December 1944 it also reveals the total number of *Grille* available for action was never lower than 161. The type remained in production until the end of the war.

In late 1944, BMM developed an advanced type of weapons carrier for the sIG 33 using the open-topped chassis of a *Jagdpanzer* 38(t) *Hetzer* (baiter). Little is known of this interesting vehicle, except that it did not enter production.

Organization and deployment

The new type of heavy self-propelled infantry gun was to be issued to the 9.Kp of the infantry regiment in both Panzer and PzGren divisions and organized according the new KStN 1120a, dated 16 January 1943. This structure emerged from an earlier KStN produced for those sIG 33 mounted on either the PzKpfw I or PzKpfw II.

Basically the unit consisted of the *Gruppe* Führer (staff platoon), the *Geschützstaffel* (gun section) with three platoons, the *Munitionsstaffel* (ammunition echelon), the *Gefechtstross* (combat train), the *Instandsetzungsgruppe* (vehicle workshop echelon) and the *Gepäcktross* (baggage train).

Gruppe Führer

The staff platoon was home of the commander. He was supplied with a *mittlere FunkPanzerwagen* (m FuPzWg – medium armoured radio car) SdKfz 251/3 to allow to him to communicate with all elements of his company, and also battalion and regimental staff. The *Richtkreis Uffizier* (NCO responsible for surveying the firing position – usually a sergeant) was also responsible setting the range of the firing position. By using reference points to determine this he could then synchronize the fire from each gun, a prerequisite for fire control.

The KStN does not refer to an observer usually considered essential for the direction of fire from a gun battery. Normally an observer would be part of an artillery battery or company and positioned adjacent to the commander of the combat elements during a firefight. A forward observer in an artillery regiment was equipped with a specialized observation vehicle, whereas the observer in a sIG unit had to work on the ground or in a vehicle near to the frontline.

Although communications on the battlefield would be by radio, the staff company had an SdKfz 251/11equipped to lay telephone cables to maintain contact with remote stations in areas with poor radio reception. The staff company also had two *Kettenkrad* (SdKfz 2) for liaison duties.

Geschützstaffel

The gun section had three platoons, and was led by a *Richtkreis Uffizier*, and was issued with an SdKfz 251/1 for the headquarters section. Also each platoon had two 15cm sIG 33 auf Gw 38 *Grille* to provide firepower. The *Geschützstaffel* also had, if available, two SdKfz 3 *Maultier* [mule] half-track trucks with *Sonderanhänger* (SdAnh – special purpose trailer) 31 to carry ammunition, a *Kübelwagen* and a *Kettenkrad* (SdKfz 2) for liaison duties.

Munitionsstaffel

The ammunition supply team was usually supplied with three *Maultier* half-track trucks and ammunition trailers – units fighting in Russia were given preference – but as an alternative, standard 3-ton trucks would be issued.

Gefechtstross

The combat train had four trucks to transport food and general supplies and to tow a field kitchen. The unit also had a *Kübelwagen* for liaison duties.

A column of vehicles from 1.Skijäger Division moving during the winter 1943/44: In the lead is a *mittlerer Schützenpanzerwagen* (SPW – armoured personnel carrier) SdKfz 251/1 which carried the platoon leader and also the *Richtkreis-Trupp* (aiming circle squad), which surveyed suitable firing positions.

Three *Grille* of Skijäger-Brigade 1 ready to fire from an open position on the snow-covered steppe; the lead vehicle is an Ausf K accompanied by two Ausf H. It was common practice to deploy a mixed establishment of the types until the end of the war.

Instandsetzungs-Gruppe

The workshop section had two trucks to transport the mechanics responsible for repair and maintenance, and also spare parts for all vehicles. The section also had a *Kübelwagen*. The recovery section was equipped with an s Zgkw 12t (SdKfz 8).

Gepäcktross

The baggage train was equipped with a single truck.

It was standard practice to always give preference for the supply of specialized vehicles, such as the *Maultier* and *Kettenkrad*, to units fighting on the Eastern Front. However, if any *Munitions-Fahrzeuge auf Gw 38* were available, these would be used to replace the *Maultier* trucks in the gun section.

Combat

In 1943, 1.PzDiv fought in the southern part of the Eastern Front. In early 1944, after being almost annihilated near Kiev, the unit was sent to Greece. It was returned to Russia in summer 1944, where the division was involved in defensive fighting around Ternopol, before retreating toward the Vistula salient. As 1944 came to an end, 1.PzDiv was deployed for the defence of Budapest. In May 1945, what remained of 1.PzDiv was captured the Red Army.

Other than PzGrenRgt 113, 1.PzDiv had a further armoured infantry regiment, PzGrenRgt 1. The 9.Kp in both regiments was issued with six 15cm sIG 33 auf Gw 38; a total of twelve.

No after action reports from sIG companies have survived. However, an interview was made with Theo Vogt, a veteran of 9./PzGrenRgt 113 in 1.PzDiv where he served as a *vorgeschobener-Beobachter* (VB – forward observer) responsible for fire control:

> Q: Was your unit also issued with the later *Grille* Ausf K (rear-mounted gun)? Did you use ammunition carriers based on the Ausf K?
>
> Vogt: No, PzGrenRgt 1 and 113 were issued with only six Ausf H, and all remained in service until the end of the war. We had no armoured ammunition carriers.
>
> Q: How do you rate (in retrospect) the *Grille* (vehicle, gun)?
>
> Vogt: The Škoda chassis and running gear was rugged, and not prone to mechanical failures. The Praga engine was reliable and robust. I cannot remember an exchange or general overhaul of this engine. During the mud period we had frequent failures of the bearings in the transverse drive shafts, or breakages of those shafts due to the considerable weight of the gun. When firing the No.6 charge [the most powerful] over longer periods, the seals in the gun recuperator began to leak.
>
> Q: How did the ammunition supply work near the front?
>
> Vogt: Initially the ammunition squad was issued with halt-tracked trucks, Ford 'Muli' (*Maultier*) with a V8 engine, but because of the flimsy suspension and small running wheels, the truck lacked mobility in heavy mud. The vehicles were often overloaded. Due to the height of the cover over the load bed, the truck could not be kept near our firing positions. For front-line supply we preferred the low and agile 1-ton half-tracked tractor [SdKfz 10], with its 100hp Maybach engine. For transport of fuel or ammunition from rear divisional or corps stores, we had one Mercedes half-tracked heavy truck and several Opel Blitz 3-ton trucks, both proven types of vehicle. From autumn 1944, we also used some US-built Studebaker six-wheel-drive trucks captured from the Russians, but these were true gas guzzlers. The large tarpaulin cover was only used during longer rest periods, or during rail transport or at night. In combat, we expected to withstand wind, rain, snow and dust.
>
> Q: Did you, being a forward observer, have your own vehicle? Were there any armoured vehicles available for a VB?
>
> Vogt: Observers and radio operators were not issued with a vehicle. The short distance to the *Beobachtung-Stelle* [BSt — observation post], often less than 1,000m, was covered on foot. Quite often, depending on the amount of ammunition flying around, we had to run. Beside the *Grille*, the only armoured vehicle in the gun platoon was an SdKfz 251/1, for the platoon leader, armed with two *Maschinengewehr* [MG — machine gun] 42 for close defence (dismountable). The VB and the radio operator travelled inside this vehicle, but near to the frontline the VB and radio operator would be close to the company commander of the *Panzergrenadiere* [PzGren — armoured infantry].
>
> Q: Which radio set did you use in the company? Did it work well?
>
> Vogt: My radio operator worked with a TornFuG 'h' [portable radio set]. This VHF radio had the transmitter and receiver in a steel casing with a removable front cover. Power

The four man crew of a *Grille* Ausf H during a break in operations to read mail from home. The commander (right) of the gun is leaning on the FuSprGer 'f' radio and is almost hidden behind the *Rundblickfernrohr* (RblF — panoramic periscope sight) 36.

supply was provided by a rechargeable battery and the range was 1 to 2.5km, depending on the terrain. In mountainous terrain we experienced large radio shadows [areas of poor contact] and here we relied on cable telephone communication. Due to enemy action such as artillery or grenade launcher fire this connection was frequently broken. Then the *Strippenflicker* (cable repairers) had to move out.

Q: How did you find the the general supply situation particularly in regard to ammunition, fuel and food?

Vogt: A clear and significant shortage of ammunition and fuel became evident in early 1945. By that time, not earlier, the destruction of our desalination works and the railway infrastructure reached a dangerous, decisive level. Often we received fuel by truck, literally at the last minute and refuelling from 20-litre fuel jerrycans took further time. The supply of food was adequate until the last days of the war. Nutrition was very limited and we often ate the same food day after day. Deliveries became even more sporadic as problems, including strafing aircraft, mounted. Often we did not receive a hot meal until midnight.

By 1943, the pre-war design of the PzKpfw 38(t) chassis for the Gw 38 had been fully developed and any weak points had been identified, assessed and resolved. The type was considered to be a more versatile and powerful self-propelled gun when compared to those mounted older PzKpfw I and PzKpfw II chassis.

It must be remembered that during the planning process for a new type of combat vehicle, the weight of many components (engine, transmission and brake system) would be known. However, during development any improvements made usually resulted in an increase in weight. This problem

A *Grille* Ausf K of 3.SS-PzDiv Totenkopf passes a convoy made up of a variety of truck types near Budapest in early 1945. The lead vehicle, a battered Krupp Protze has broken down due to a mechanical failure. Note the tracks on the *Grille* have been fitted with ice cleats [spuds].

would affect almost all German armoured fighting vehicles produced in World War II.

A prime example is the PzKpfw IV; as it was developed from Ausf B through to Ausf G, the weight increased by 33 percent, which significantly led to a 28 percent decrease in the power-to-weight ratio.

The installation of a heavy infantry gun on standard tank chassis could overload the engine, transmission, brakes and cooling system and also many other mechanical components. The self-propelled gun with the best power-to-weight ratio was the15cm sIG 33/1 auf Gw 38(t) *Grille*.

As an infantry gun, the heavy calibre 15cm sIG 33 was somewhat unique as no other army regularly deployed such weapon on the frontline, preferring instead to use the grenade launcher [mortar]. One, the 120mm M 1938 heavy grenade launcher used by the Red Army was a remarkable weapon and so good that any captured were used by German forces [designated GrWrf 378(r)] against the Soviets. Later the Germans decided copy it as the 12cm *schwere Granatwerfer* (s GrWrf) 42.

However, the 15cm sIG 33 offered a greater range of applications and although the impact of a 15cm shell was devastating it also had a demoralizing effect on troops. Both the towed and self-propelled 15cm sIG 33 remained in service until end of the war.

In early 1942, as efforts to introduce self-propelled guns into the rifle and artillery regiments in Panzer divisions, so the situation for the supply of prime movers worsened. On 12 May 1942, *Heeresgruppe Süd* (Army Group South) reported a number of problems with the establishment of new units and re-equipping others:

A *Wespe* travels across the vast, open Russian steppe as the snow begins to melt in spring 1944. The retreating Red Army has abandoned a 45mm M1942 (M-42) anti-tank gun, which at the time was being replaced in front-line service, by the far more effective 57mm M1943 (ZiS-2).

Establishment of motorized formations and army troops are being severely affected by the shortage of prime movers, especially the number of available heavy tractors, which is by no means sufficient. This situation forces us to take the following steps:

1) From now on, heavy artillery battalions equipped with batteries of four guns each will be supplied with only three s ZgKw. This measure will require strict organization with every change of positions or longer transfer marches.
2) The *Brückenbau-Kompanien* [bridge-building companies] earmarked for re-equipment will receive only 50 percent of 2) the allotted tractors; instead trucks will be issued.
3) To mobilize the newly issued heavy anti-tank guns all available tractors of foreign manufacture will be utilized.
4) For *Heeresgruppe Süd*, a full mobilization can be achieved this way. The Führer has ordered that agricultural tractors will be tested to tow anti-tank guns and light-artillery pieces. If these are successful, all tractors produced for agricultural usage will be diverted to the military.

In November 1942, OrgAbt urged the use of the new *Raupenschlepper Ost* (RSO – fully tracked carrier: East) as a towing vehicle for light and medium anti-tank guns or artillery pieces. But the RSO was not an effective prime mover, being too light and also unstable when cornering. In desperation, they even suggested that trucks should be used.

Panzerartillerie

For the Panzer divisions, January 1943 should be seen as a turning point in the search for mobile artillery.

In late 1941, the *Schützen* (motorized rifle) regiments had received a small number (due to economic constraints) of 15cm sIG 33 self-propelled guns. However, since this first deployment was successful, military planners showed more enthusiasm for the type. From 1943 onwards, the sIG 33 mounted on the Gw 38(t) would become standard equipment for the *Schützen* regiments.

The first attempt to construct a self-propelled gun using only German-manufactured components was achieved when a test series of 10.5cm leFH 18/1 auf Gw IVb was completed in January 1942. The guns left the factory in February 1942, and a battery was established with 16.PzDiv in September for trials under combat conditions. Unfortunately, as yet no further information on the combat trials has been found.

A self-propelled gun specifically designed for artillery regiments attached to the Panzer divisions was still not available.

In July 1942 the OrgAbt reported:

To continue the improvement of our self-propelled guns, GenStbdH orders the development of a self-propelled gun by mounting a leFH 18 on a PzKpfw IV chassis.

However a letter dated 20 April 1943, details the development of Sfl:

Reference: Sfl

1) *Leichte* Sfl

Subject of the research was to mount the *leichte Feldhaubitze* 18 on the chassis of a *Heuschrecke* [locust] type vehicle. After an obvious misunderstanding, these experiments will now be carried out using the complete gun assembly from the Sfl IVb built by Krupp, for installation in the *Heuschrecke*. For this purpose, WaPrüf 4 [the bureau responsible for artillery weapons] will dispatch one Sfl IVb to Krupp-Grusson Werke at Magdeburg. The turret including gun will then be sent to Essen to be used as one component for the ten *Heuschrecke* under construction.

2) 15cm Sfl

An examination has shown that installation of the unaltered sFH 18 gun will encounter great difficulties. After consideration of all options, the only remaining objective is to carry on the work as follows:

The ongoing development of the 15cm sFH 43 and the 12.8cm K for mounting as a self-propelled gun has continued by using as many components of the sFH 18 as possible. This has the advantage of being able to rely on an already existing gun type. After examining the wooden mock-up for a *Grille* mounting a 15cm gun, it was decided that the gun must be moved to the rear, dismounting the gun will be achieved by using lifting

The staff sections in self-propelled artillery units were provided with *mittlerer Funkpanzerwagen* (m FuPzWg — medium radio vehicle) SdKfz 251/3, fitted with Fu 8, Fu 5 and FuSprech 'f' radios. Here an SdKfz 251/3, from 16.PzDiv, is fitted with a 1.4m *Sternantenne* (star antenna) 'd' rather than the standard 2m rod antenna.

The ammunition-supply echelons were normally issued with four-wheel-drive trucks. In early 1943, units on the Eastern Front began to receive *Maultier* (mule) half-tracked trucks to provide better mobility in mud and snow. The equipment could be fitted on a number of different types including the Ford V 3000 3-ton truck. However, due to the fragility of the Carden-Lloyd bogie, the payload had to be reduced to 2 tons.

beams mounted on the idler wheels. For practical experience, preliminary trials will be made using the 4b chassis delivered from Magdeburg.

3) ...

4) The design of a self-propelled gun using the sFH 43 will be carried on regardless of those items noted above.

The notes show that work on a successor to the 10.5cm leFH 18/2 auf Gw IVb would continue and a dismountable main gun would be the requirement for all ongoing development of the *Heuschrecke*. Both Krupp and Rheinmetall were ordered to deliver their prototypes for the self-propelled gun for field trials. However, the proposed type would never be mass produced.

The proposal to develop a self-propelled chassis for both a 12.8cm flat trajectory gun and the improved 15cm sFH 43 emerged at the same time as that for the 10.5cm leFH 18/2. It was also proposed to construct a dual-purpose self-propelled gun using components of the new PzKpfw V Panther, but only wooden models were produced (*Grille* 15).

10.5cm leFH 18 self-propelled gun

In early 1942, *Waffenamt* department WaPrüf 4 produced a number of specifications for future self-propelled guns; the ultimate goal was for all types to be fitted with a fully rotatable turret and also have the facility to dismount the gun. Possibly this was the reason for the cancellation of the *Geschützwagen* IVb project, as it did not have a rotatable turret or a dismountable gun. It must be remembered that in 1942, German forces were fighting battles on the Eastern Front and in the deserts of North Africa and any disruption to the production of the PzKpfw IV tank was officially forbidden.

10.5cm leFH 18/2 auf Gw II *Wespe*

Due to the seriousness of the situation on the battlefront a number of interim solutions were ordered. For a self-propelled light artillery gun, consideration was given to the chassis of the PzKpfw II and also the PzKpfw 38(t). The latter had been selected as the chassis on which to mount a 7.62cm PaK 36(r), a 7.5cm PaK 40 and also the 15cm sIG 33 and it was thought impossible to increase in production.

The PzKpfw II chassis had already been proven inadequate when mounted with a heavy gun. The many negative experiences with the 15cm sIG 33 auf PzKpfw II been forgotten and Alkett was contracted to develop the chassis to mount a 10.5cm leFH 18/2.

The military planners decided that a full conversion would be required to carry the heavy gun. The fighting compartment was to be located at the rear to

10.5cm leFH 18/2 auf Gw II *Wespe*

Calibre	10.5cm
Ammunition stowage	30 rounds
Elevation	-5 to +42°
Traverse	20° to each side
Firing height	n/a
Combat weight	11t
Performance	140hp
Speed (maximum)	40kph
Range (road/cross country)	140/95km
Crew	Four
Radio equipment	FuSprecht 'f'
Production	676 SP guns 159 ammo carrier

Two *Grille* Ausf H in an open position ready to supply supporting fire; on the wide open landscape of the Russian steppe such a unit would be in imminent danger of an attack by enemy aircraft or artillery. The ability to quickly advance or retreat was vital. The white helmet symbol stencilled on the side of the superstructure indicates that they are in service with PzGrenRgt Grossdeutschland (GD).

allow easy access, which required the engine to be repositioned in the centre of the hull. After the first prototype had been completed it became obvious that the hull had to be lengthened.

The new *Geschützwagen* II (Gw II – weapon carrier) was fitted with the running gear from a PzKpfw II Ausf F and also the same 140hp Maybach HL 62 TR petrol engine driving a slightly modified ZF SSG 46 transmission.

The Ursus facility in Warsaw was contracted to manufacture the new vehicle, which became known as *Wespe* (wasp). The *Rüststand* statistics, published in December 1943, note that 200 of the type had to be delivered by the end of April, and from then on produced at a rate of 20 a month. (At the same time, Hitler was finalizing his plans for his great offensive on the Kursk salient.)

The production target was not achieved until the end of June 1943, when Ursus had delivered a total of 239 *Wespe* which were accepted by WaPrüf 4 and then delivered to various units. In the same month it was planned for a *Munitionsträger* (ammunition carrier) *Wespe* to enter production. It is most likely that production did not begin immediately as there was just sufficient capacity to assemble the *Wespe*. However, the factory did manage to complete 10 ammunition carriers by the end of June: Not the 60 originally planned.

An officer supervises the crew of an *Grille* Ausf H as they practice handling a massive 15cm *Stielgranate* 42 hollow-charge round. The weapon, designed to defeat enemy heavy armour, was simply attached to the gun barrel before a special charge was fired to ignite the shell's propellant.

Forward observers of PzGrenRgt 113 (1.PzDiv) in position: The observer is scanning the battlefield with binoculars, while his radio operator uses a *Tornister Funkgerät* d2 portable radio to keep in contact with the battery commander.

But on 15 July 1943, WaPrüf 4 sent a terse note to a Dr Bankwitz of Krupp:

> *Hauptman* Mass of WaPrüf 4 reports that the *Wespe* (10.5cm auf PzKpfw II), which was designed by Alkett did not prove to be satisfactory despite its appealing appearance. Production will be cancelled. Mass asks to keep this matter confidential.

In February 1944, it was officially confirmed that production of the *Wespe* would cease after the initial order was completed. It was not until January 1944 that exact production numbers were released, and before this date only those vehicles accepted by WaPrüf 4 were shown. A total of 676 *Wespe* had been produced including 159 ammunition carriers.

The 1944 statistics also show the number of vehicles being returned to Ursus for repair or refurbished. Between January and September 1944, a total of 47 *Wespe* and three *Munitionsträger* were repaired and accepted by the ordnance office. The *Frontverbrauch* (losses in combat) data was also shown; in 1943 some 63 vehicles were lost, and 311 in 1944. A peak was reached April 1944, when 72 were reported as lost. In the same period some 43 ammunition carriers were also lost.

The number of damaged *Wespe*, which were returned to combat by front-line workshops by cannibalizing ammunition carriers, remains unknown. Production of the *Wespe* ceased in June 1944, but the proposed replacement, the *Heuschrecke*, was not to be built.

15cm sFH 18/1 auf Gw IV *Hummel*

Initially there were no definite plans to produce a heavy self-propelled gun to fulfill a number of future *Waffenamt* proposals. However in early summer 1943, the 15cm sFH 18 began to be examined by planners.

As early as 21 March 1943, the OrgAbt reported on the efforts to develop and produce a 12.8cm gun rather than the 15cm sFH 43 originally intended to supersede the sFH 18. The new low-trajectory field gun would be produced as a towed and also a self-propelled gun, and replace the s 10cm K 18 as soon as possible. The mainstay of German artillery forces, the 15cm sFH 18 would remain in production basically unchanged, but maximum range would increase to 15,000m by firing special ammunition. After a series of discussions it was decided to fit the gun with a muzzle brake: the sFH 18 M.

A self-propelled vehicle was to be designed and developed to mount the 12.8cm gun or the 15cm sFH 18. But neither project could be realized in time.

Once again a simple solution was sought and Rheinmetall-Borsig in Duisburg and Alkett began the development work. The main requirement was to use as many components as possible from current tanks, but without affecting production. The resulting vehicle was designated as the *Geschützwagen* III/IV.

The hull especially designed and fabricated for the type slightly longer than that of the PzKpfw IV. A 265hp Maybach HL 120 TRM engine was fitted in the centre of the hull, creating space for a large open-topped fighting compartment

When production of the *Grille* Ausf H ended, the completely redesigned Ausf K entered service. The new type had the engine mounted in the centre of the hull with the driver seated alongside. The gun was moved to the rear and mounted in a larger fighting compartment which had much improved rear access.

15cm sFH 18/1 auf Gw III/IV *Hummel*

Calibre	15cm
Ammunition stowage	18 rounds
Elevation	-3 to +42°
Traverse	15° to each side
Combat weight	22t
Performance	265hp
Speed (maximum)	42kph
Range (road/cross country)	215/130km
Crew	Four
Radio equipment	FuSprecht 'f'
Production	705 SP guns 157 carriers

to be mounted on the rear. The running gear from a PzKpfw IV was used, but both the ZF SSG 77 transmission and the final-drive sprocket came from a PzKpfw III. A spade to absorb the recoil forces of the howitzer was not fitted.

In service the 10.5cm leFH 18/1 self-propelled gun became known as the *Hummel* (bumble bee). An ammunitions carrier was produced using the same chassis.

Initially the 15cm sFH 18/1 gun was fitted with a massive muzzle brake in an attempt to reduce recoil forces when firing special ammunition. However, after a series of trials the muzzle brake was removed and never fitted on production vehicles. This meant that the most powerful propellant used was a *Ladung* 8 (charge No.8), which gave a range of 13,250m.

Production

On 15 February 1943, the new self-propelled chassis for the 15cm sFH 18 *Hummel* and the 8.8cm PaK 43/41 (*Hornisse* – hornet) were presented to the Führer. All pre-production testing had been successful, and a delighted Adolf Hitler ordered production to commence almost immediately. In October 1943, it was estimated that 120 units could be produced each month with 66 percent as anti-tank guns, and 33 percent as artillery guns.

In February 1943, after a delay of four weeks, the first five *Hummel* were accepted by the *Waffenamt* and a total of 333 had been produced by the end of 1943.

In May 1943, it was ordered that 25 percent of *Hummel* output was to be completed as armoured ammunition carriers, and by the end of the year 96 had

A *Grille* Ausf H on a parade through a small town on the Normandy coast in early 1943 passes a senior officer taking the salute from a Steyr 1500, command car. The badge on the vehicle, a black sword on a white shield, identifies the unit as PzGrenRgt 9 of 26.PzDiv.

been produced. *Rüststand* statistics report that 60 *Hummel* and 12 ammunition carriers were lost in combat during 1943.

Production figures for 1944 show that 289 *Hummel* and 61 ammunition carriers were completed. However, some 250 self-propelled guns and 66 ammunition carriers had been lost in action

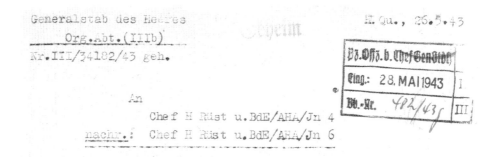

This document shows the prime establishment with *Wespe* and *Hummel* self-propelled guns to various units.

In March 1945, approximately 50 *Hummel* were delivered to front-line units. But on 9 March, production at Duisburg was halted after Allied bombers all but destroyed the factory; a note from the *Waffenamt* states that 250 *Hummel* were on the production line. A further 199 completed hulls were ready for collection from Mülheim. Discussions began immediately on the feasibility of relocating final production to the *Nibelungenwerke* in Austria.

Armoured Observation Vehicles

With the introduction of modern artillery it became obvious that the clear and reliable transmission of information was indispensable to artillery commanders. In World War I, the forward observer had to rely on a horse or his feet to get to his position, and often operated close to the front-line units he was supposed to support. Since in the first instance, a forward observer relied on the telephone or a dispatch rider to send communications, there would always be a problem: any delay between making an observation and opening fire could have fatal consequences. While this approach was sufficient for the needs of the light artillery, for the long-range heavy artillery better solutions were being sought.

The '*vorgeschobener Beobachter*' (VB – forward observer), was usually a member of a front-line combat troop in order to provide target information to get supporting fire from the local commander.

PzGrenLehrRgt 901, equipped with *Grille* Ausf H, was one of many training units to be amalgamated with Panzer-Lehr-Division in February 1944. The vehicle carries a German-style 'L' to indicate that it is in service with PzLehrDiv; the origin of the diamond symbol is unknown.

Unlike all other German tanks in service, the driver of a PzKpfw 38(t) was positioned on the right-hand side of the chassis. On a *Grille* Ausf K this was a separate compartment fabricated from welded armour plate.

To improve the performance of the artillery, the *Wehrmacht* introduced specialized equipment for forward observers at the beginning of World War II. Understandably efficient radio equipment was considered to be essential for modern artillery forces. But specialized observer tanks were not yet available, so a vehicle such as a passenger car had to be adopted for this purpose.

With establishment of the first tank divisions in the German Reich, the requirement for a new type of observation vehicle was given utmost importance. The type should be capable of keeping pace with the leading echelons of a rapidly advancing Panzer division, while being sufficiently armoured and installed with reliable radio equipment. In 1940, the first *Panzerbeobachtungswagen* (PzBeobWg – observation tank) had been developed and issued to the VBs in Panzer divisions.

In January 1941, the OKH issued their set of requirements:

- The PzBeobWg must be able to match the speed of the Panzer division.
- The type must resemble the tanks, but only be armed with MG.
- It must be provided with a radio which has a voice range of at least 15km.
- The battalion staff will be issued with three PzBeobWg, the regimental staff and the batteries with two PzBeobWg each.

SdKfz 265

In 1940, the first units were equipped with *kleiner Panzerbefehlswagen* (kl PzBefWg – light command tank) based on a PzKpfw I and designated

In 1944, the chassis of the le PzJg 38(t) *Hetzer* (baiter) was chosen for the development of a number of support vehicles. One type mounted a 15cm sIG 33 installed in a sleek-looking armoured superstructure, but it did not progress beyond the prototype stage.

SdKfz 265. Originally these vehicles were issued to the commander of a tank company. But when sufficient command tanks based on the PzKpfw III became available to replace the kl PzBefWg, a number of these were issued to the artillery regiments in a Panzer division. However, a uniform method of equipping units was not possible at that time. Since the kl PzBefWg was fitted with radio equipment that worked on the *Panzerwaffe* frequency band, communications from an observer were received directly by the artillery fire-direction centre.

SdKfz 253

The *leichter gepanzerter Beobachtungskraftwagen* (le gep BeobKw – light armoured observation vehicle) was a originally designed for the forward observers of *Sturmartillerie* (assault artillery) units. The vehicle had a fully enclosed armoured hull which provided protection from armour-piercing bullets.

The SdKfz 253 carried a crew of four, an officer observer, an NCO observer, a driver and a radio operator. Initially only the *Sturmgeschütz* units were supplied with the type, but in 1941 they began to be issued to the artillery regiments in Panzer divisions.

All le gep BeobKw issued to *Sturmgeschütz* units were fitted with a Fu 15 and Fu 16 radio installation. When issued to artillery units, combinations of either Fu 8 and Fu 4, or Fu 12 and FuSprech 'f' were fitted. Variations were possible, and these depended on the supply and the requirements of commanders in the field. Also carried was a portable TornFuGer 'g' radio, which allowed the observers to dismount on the battlefront.

Components of the SdKfz 253 were later used to create the *leichter gepanzerter Schützenpanzerwagen*, (le gep SPW – light armoured rifle team carrier), the later SdKfz 250 series.

SdKfz 254

In 1936, Saurer had begun to manufacture an unusual wheel-cum-track vehicle for the Austrian army. After the *Anschluss*, the company came under German control and their vehicle came to the notice of the *Waffenamt*. The RK 7 version was evaluated and fitted with an armoured superstructure, sufficiently large to house a *Beobachtungstrupp* (observation team) of four and the required equipment. Designated *mittlerer gepanzerter Beobachtungskraftwagen* (m gep BeobKw – medium armoured observation vehicle), the vehicle was intended to be a supplement to the SdKfz 253 equipping various Panzer divisions. A production order was issued by the *Waffenamt* for 140, units of which 128 entered service.

The SdKfz 254 carried the same equipment as the SdKfz 253. In early 1941, most artillery regiments attached to Panzer divisions were issued with between six and 15 of the SdKfz 253 or 254 PzBeobwg.

Krupp-Gruson Werke built the *Heuschrecke* (locust) which was designed so that the turret could be dismounted from the chassis. Only one was built before the project was cancelled in favour of more conventional types.

SdKfz 250/5

When production of the open-topped SdKfz 250 began it was decided to halt production of the SdKfz 253. Another reason was that the commander of a *Sturmartillerie* unit was now supplied with an assault gun.

The SdKfz 250/5 variant was a *Beobachtungskraftwagen* (observation vehicle) which, unlike the SdKfz 252 and SdKfz 254, was issued on a regular

Radio	Fu 5	Fu 2	Fu 8	Fu 4	FuSprechGer 'f'	TornFuGer 'g'
Type	UKW receiver 'e' and 10W transmitter 'c'	UKW receiver 'e'	MW receiver 'c' and 30W transmitter 'a'	MW receiver 'c'	Combined transmitter and receiver	Combined transmitter and receiver
Frequency	Ultrashort Wave	Ultrashort Wave	Medium Wave	Medium Wave	Ultrashort Wave	Ultrashort Wave
Range (voice)	Static 5km Moving 5km	Static 5km Moving 3km	Static 40km Moving 15km	Static 40km Moving 15km	Static 6–8km Moving 5–6km	Normal 12km Lying with low antenna 6km Range at night 50%
Weight	7.5kg	7.5kg	7.5kg	7.5kg	7.5kg	18.3kg
Application	*Panzertruppe*	*Panzertruppe*	*Artillerie & Panzerartillerie*	*Artillerie & Panzerartillerie*	*Panzeraufklärer Panzergrenadiere Panzerartillerie*	Portable radio for *Panzeraufklärer Panzergrenadiere Panzerartillerie*

basis to reconnaissance elements of various units, including PzKpfw VI Tiger battalions.

When used by the artillery, the majority of vehicles were fitted with Fu 8 and Fu 4, plus an optional FuSprechGer 'f', but a Fu 12 and FuSprechGer 'f' was also used. The FuSprechGer 'f' was normally used for communications between a forward observer and a *Batterie-Offizier* (BttrOffz – battery officer). This radio was also used to communicate directly with the self-propelled guns.

When a FuSprechGer 'f' was out of the voice range (5km), a Fu 8 (which had a range of 20km), was used. Also a TornFuGer 'g', portable radio was carried in the vehicle.

A New Observation Tank

When the development of improved self-propelled artillery for the Panzer divisions began, military planners also recognized the requirement for tracked observation vehicles having the same mobility as a tank over poor terrain.

In 1941, German artillery relied on a number of observation vehicles. Originally built for the Austrian army, the Saurer RK 7 a complex wheel-cum-track vehicle was adopted by the *Wehrmacht* as a *mittlerer gepanzerter Beobachtungswagen* (m gep BeobKw – medium armoured observation vehicle) and designated SdKfz 254. The vehicle shown is from PzArtRgt 102 in 9.PzDiv.

A specification was written for an observation tank based on a current main battle tank.

In 1942, the PzKpfw V Panther medium tank was under development to fulfill the requirements of the battered and stressed tank divisions. As development progressed, military planners conceived the idea of creating a 'family' of support tanks by using the chassis of the more technically advanced PzKpfw V Panther as a base. One such type to be ordered was a tank fitted with sophisticated observation equipment.

By utilizing the Panther chassis the type would have the same level of armour protection and superior mobility. To create more space inside the turret for observation and extra radio equipment, the 7.5cm L/70 gun was removed and replaced with a dummy fabricated from wood.

The turret was equipped with an *Entfernungsmesser* 1.25m (EM – range-finder) manufactured by Zeiss installed in the front plate. Also fitted was a *Turmbeobachtungsfernrohr* (TBF – turret observation periscope) 2, a *Turmsehrohr* (TSR – commander's periscope) 1, and also a *Scherenfernrohr* (SF – scissors-type periscope).

But once again the dire situation in the German armaments industry did not allow the type to enter series production. Instead it was decided to produce a less sophisticated observation tank.

Panzerbeobachtungswagen III

In order to produce the desperately needed observation tank, it was decided to fit

A *Grille* Ausf H covered in foliage, in an attempt to prevent being spotted by patrolling enemy aircraft: the next vehicle follows at a distance of 100m. Before going into action, the branches would be removed.

observation equipment in refurbished PzKpfw III tanks. Subsequently this simple solution was accepted by the *Waffenamt* and the type entered service in 1943.

The *Waffenamt* decided that only refurbished Ausf G and Ausf H variants of the PzKpfw III were to be used for conversion and contracted Alkett for the work. To create the extra space required, the 5cm gun was removed and replaced with a replica made from wood. The only armament fitted was a single *Maschinengewehr* (MG – machine gun) 34 for close defence: the MG 34 in the hull was replaced by a pistol port.

A TBF 2 observation periscope was fitted in the roof of the turret, as was a mounting for a SF scissors-type periscope and a TSR 1 commander's periscope was fitted near to the cupola.

The new space in the interior was similar to that of a of the PzBefWg III command tank, but the PzBeobWg III, had a Fu 8 and Fu 4 artillery-type radio installation. The vehicle also carried a FuSprechGer 'f' and a TornFuGer 'g' portable radio.

On 2 September 1943, OrgAbt ordered that additional Fu 5 radio sets were to be issued:

> To improve the communication between tank and other units, provision with radio sets will be broadened. They will be issued to all PzBeobWg auf PzKpfw III with regimental and battalion staffs. The self-propelled gun batteries will receive an additional Fu 5.

It is not known how these additional radios were delivered.

The PzBeobWg III was the first of the type to utilize a standard tank chassis. The gun was replicated by a simple steel tube and a *Maschinengewehr* (MG — machine gun) 34 mounted in the centre of the gun mantlet for self-defence. The type was fitted with extensive radio and observation equipment.

In February 1943, the conversion of PzBeobwg III began at the same facilities that were producing the *Wespe* and *Hummel*. Production continued until April 1944 when some 262 units had been completed. A *Rüststand* statistic reported that from August 1943 to August 1944 there had been a monthly stock of 110 to a maximum of 162 vehicles with front-line units. From September 1943, the stock was significantly decreased.

The PzBeobWg III was issued to artillery regiments in Panzer divisions. A KStN dated January 1943, notes that two of the type were issued to the *Wespe* batteries, three to the *Hummel* batteries, and the self-propelled gun battalion staff and the regimental staff received one each. But a KStN details the authorized numbers which in many instances were purely theoretical. Amalgamated organizational forms showing the distribution of SdKfz 250/5 and PzBeobWg III were accepted as correct.

On 16 May 1943, the OrgAbt sent a report to the office of the Inspector General of the Armoured Forces:

> A steady but variable percentage will be taken out of tank and armoured half-track production to deliver observer vehicles for the artillery. We also accept that there is a necessity to provide these to the forward observers and the *Artillerie-Verbindungskommando* [AVK - artillery liaison detachment]. However, due to the shortage of armoured vehicles and their high fuel consumption we urge you to limit the number proposed for the *Panzerartillerie* to be kept to the absolute minimum necessary. Therefore we suggest you issue three armoured observer's vehicles to the AVK and three

In 1942, the open-topped SdKfz 250/5 was replaced by the fully enclosed SdKfz 253. Both were designated as le gep BeobKw, and were fitted with virtually identical radio and optical equipment.

A *Hummel* in the final
assembly hall at Deutsche
Eisenwerke, Duisburg:
A 15cm sFH 18 gun is
lifted into position in the
fighting compartment
before the front parts of the
superstructure are fitted.

for the VBs of a Panzer division. These vehicles will be part of the PzArtAbt, which relies on cooperation with the PzRgt.

The almost unsolvable problem of supplying the Panzer divisions is caused by the shortage of trucks and underlines the need to reduce the allocation of tracked vehicles. If, as initially planned, nine observation tanks were to be issued to each Panzer division then the majority of their missions will be to operate as radio stations.

On 9 June, SS-PzGrenDiv Das Reich received nine PzBeobWg III, clearly contradicting concerns expressed by the OrgAbt. Since four le gep BeobKw (SdKfz 250/5) were also issued, it meant that 13 armoured observer vehicles would become the standard for *Wehrmacht*, Waffen-SS also for Panzer Divisions and Panzer Grenadier Divisions.

On 4 July 1943, in contrast to the previously alarming message from the OrgAbt, the GenStbdH sent a report to the *Chef Heeresrüstung* (Chief of Army Equipment):

We request you provide the artillery regiments in Panzer divisions according to the following standards:
Artillery regiments with a self-propelled battalion:
Nine PzBeobWg III
Four PzBeobWg (SdKfz 250/5)

Artillery regiments without a self-propelled battalion:
13 PzBeobWg (SdKfz 250/5)

The PzKpfw II chassis proved to be suitable for mounting a 10.5cm leFH 18. The engine was relocated to the centre of the hull which, in turn, allowed a large fighting compartment to be fitted on the rear. The vehicle has been positioned behind a line of trees to take advantage of the high-trajectory howitzer.

When self-propelled guns and PzBeobWg auf PzKpfw III are issued to Panzer divisions for the first time, all surplus SdKfz 250/5 will be handed over to other PzArtRgt to compensate for a lack of vehicles.

The observation tanks of the *Panzerartillerie* were normally equipped with the Fu 8 and also a Fu 4 radio (two medium wave receivers and one 30W transmitter, see table). A FuSprech 'f' transmitter/receiver and a TornFuGer 'g' portable radio were also carried.

This selection of radio equipment brought problems for the artillery regiment in a Panzer division, especially for the self-propelled gun battalion since the medium wave radios did not allow any direct communication with the Panzer regiment. Following reports from the front-line units, the GenStbdH ordered remedial action as evidenced in this letter dated 2 September 1943:

The communication between Panzer units and attached support units is vital, and requires an improvement in the radio equipment fitted. We therefore ask to issue the following:

An additional Fu 5 radio for all PzBeobWg auf PzKpfw III issued to staff of the self-propelled regiment, the self-propelled battalion and the self-propelled batteries. Racks have to be fabricated which can carry a Fu 8 (medium wave receiver and one 30W transmitter), alternatively a Fu 5 (ultra-short wave receiver and a 10W transmitter) or a Fu 4 (medium wave receiver) and also a FuSprech 'f'.

A number of *Hummel* self-propelled guns in various stages of completion in the final assembly hall of Deutsche Eisenwerke at their facility in Duisburg. Production was almost halted after a series of heavy bombing raids by Allied air forces.

In February 1943, the prototype of the *Hummel* was demonstrated to Adolf Hitler and senior officers from the *Waffenamt*. Originally the gun was fitted with a muzzle brake, but it was later decided to remove the item. Note the thread for the muzzle remains visible on the gun.

New PzBeobWg III on the production line or ready for delivery would be fitted with the above at the factory. For PzBeobWg III (and any SdKfz 250/5 that remained) which were in service with front-line units, the new radios would be fitted at field workshops.

On 7 November 1943, the *General der Artillerie* complained of the inadequate supply of observation tanks:

Equipping with PzBeobWg III

1) Available PzBeobWg in the army:

Operational	: 57
Under repair	: 41
Total	: 98

2) For self-propelled regiments authorized to have nine PzBeobWg, the target is 324 vehicles.

3) Shortfall: 226. The 17 artillery regiments being issued with self-propelled battalions have no PzBeobWg.

4) Due to the present situation, a full establishment of PzBeobWg will not be feasible. The

> GenInspPzTrp agrees with the decision to the issue only four PzBeobWg to each regiment. In this case it is essential that these must be based on new production vehicles and should be of the same type as issued to the Panzer Regiment.

Obviously, his demand would be almost impossible to fulfill.

In late 1943, ten *Heeres-Artillerie-Regimenter* (HArtRgt – army artillery regiments) were organized at army troop level for deployment at points of main effort and were issued with self-propelled artillery; eight issued with three *Hummel* batteries; two with two *Wespe* batteries and one further *Hummel* battery.

In January 1944, the *General der Artillerie* wrote a note of complaint:

> At present a number of HArtRgt will be converted to *Hummel*. For material reasons, these cannot be provided in the same manner as a self-propelled battalion of the Panzer divisions, in particular the PzBeobWg are in short supply. These units cannot be deployed as *Panzer-Begleit-Abteilungen* [PzBeglAbt – escort battalion] in tank regiments; they are basically a sFH battalion having better winter mobility.

His concern shows the importance of armoured observation vehicles, which were indispensable for highly mobile tank divisions. In the reality of the 1944 battlefront, a large offensive operation by tanks was virtually impossible, the *Panzertruppe* tactics now relied on limited counterattacks and wherever possible active defence.

Panzerbeobachtungswagen IV

At the end of PzBeobWg III production, military planners proposed the conversion of refurbished PzKpfw IV. However, usage of rebuilt tanks was not popular with the artillery, whose PzBeobWg III failed frequently because of their worn out drive train components.

The decision was made it to use new PzKpfw IV currently in production at Nibelungenwerke in St Valetin Anton, Austria. In January 1944, the GenArt announced that the first prototype for the PzBeobWg IV was ready for trials. At the beginning of April, it was decided that 4 percent of PzKpfw IV production was to be converted. A total of 133 PzBeobWg IV had been completed by the end of the war.

The only external difference to a standard PzKpfw IV was that a *Sturmgeschütz*-type commander's cupola was fitted on the turret. However, it is possible that some retained the original turret cupola; the reason for this is unknown.

Apart from the Fu 8, Fu 4 and FuSprechGer 'f' radio equipment, the type was fitted with a TSR (commander's periscope) and a SF (scissors-type

periscope). A TBF 2 (turret observation periscope) was not installed, possibly because the 7.5cm KwK L/48 gun was retained. Thus the question of efficient armament for observation tanks was finally resolved.

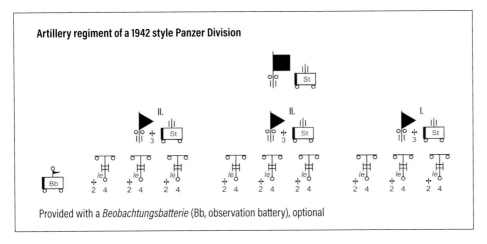

Artillery regiment of a 1942 style Panzer Division

Provided with a *Beobachtungsbatterie* (Bb, observation battery), optional

Organization

The new self-propelled artillery guns, *Wespe* and *Hummel*, were considered to be only a temporary solution. Despite this both types were quickly integrated into the artillery regiments of the Panzer divisions, and later PzGrenDiv.

In 1942, a PzArtReg of a standard tank division was issued with two light battalions equipped with 24 10.5cm leFH 18; a heavy battalion with four s 10cm K 18 and eight 15cm sFH 18.

As self-propelled guns began to arrive for front-line units in mid-1943, orders were given to convert one of the two light artillery battalions in a Panzer division into a *gemischte Artillerie-Abteilung* [Sfl] (gem ArtAbt – mixed self-propelled artillery battalion), as detailed in preliminary organizational structures.

Panzer Division 43

The new Panzer Division 43 structure incorporated the new self-propelled weapons.

I.Abt: A mixed artillery battalion with 12 10.5cm leFH 18 (Sfl) *Wespe* and six 12.8cm sFH 18 (Sfl) *Hummel*.

II.Abt: A conventional light artillery battalion equipped with 12 10.5cm leFH 18 *Wespe*.

III.Abt: This battalion was equipped with eight 15cm sFH 18 field howitzers and four 10cm s K 18 flat trajectory guns.

Initially, the plan for the future was to provide III.Abt with 18 15cm sFH 18 (Sfl) *Hummel*. In this case I.Abt would only have three batteries of *Wespe*.

Left: Elements of a PzArtRgt loaded on railway wagons awaiting transport to the frontline. Behind the 10.5cm leFH 18 *Wespe* are six 15cm sFH 18 *Hummel* and all have been covered with waterproof tarpaulins.

The four flat-trajectory fire 10cm s K 18 would be attached under the direct command of the regimental staff.

These far-reaching ideas could not be realized on a large scale, and exceptions to the rules given in the PzDiv 43 structure were widespread. For instance in March 1943, 1.PzDiv was selected to implement a trial structure with an additional gem ArtAbt (Sfl), thus doubling the number of SP guns in the unit: again this was not realized. However in 1944, 1.PzDiv had three *Hummel*

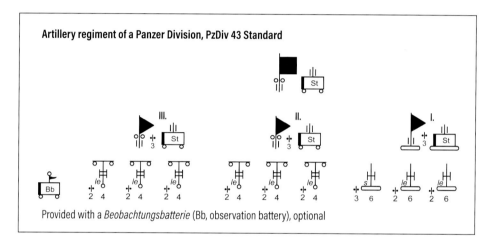

Artillery regiment of a Panzer Division, PzDiv 43 Standard

Provided with a *Beobachtungsbatterie* (Bb, observation battery), optional

The space for a driver in a *Wespe* was relatively small and was protected by a heavy visor to which was attached a vision device for when the vehicle was in action. The superstructure was fabricated from 10mm armour plate, but this only protected the crew from shrapnel and armour-piercing bullets fired by infantry.

A number of *Hummel* self-propelled guns parked in the factory yard at Deutsche Eisenwerke awaiting *Waffenamt* acceptance before being delivered to front-line units.

batteries, and 19.PzDiv one *Wespe* and two *Hummel* batteries. One exception to the rule was 21.PzDiv; the unit was, as a temporary measure, entirely equipped with French-built material.

Other support units such as *Beobachtungs-Batterien* (observation batteries) were not issued to all units. *Flugabwehrkanone* (FlaK – anti-aircraft gun) elements were issued on an irregular basis. However, these differences were possibly deliberately ordered by the divisional or regimental staff.

Panzer-Grenadier-Division 43

The new PzGrenDiv 43 basically had the same provision with artillery. However, the I.Abt had three batteries each with four 10.5cm le FH 18 *Wespe*, but no 15cm sFH 18 *Hummel* were delivered.

Panzer Division 44

With implementation of the new structure for PzDiv 44, the dire material situation was taken account. The II.*leichte Abteilung* (leAbt – light battalion) was reorganized to having two batteries with six 10.5cm leFH 18 each, instead of three batteries of four guns each. Although the number of guns remained unchanged, the requirement for soft-skinned vehicles and other support material was reduced.

Panzer-Grenadier-Division 44

In line with that of PzDiv 44, the new organizational structure for the armoured infantry saw changes to the artillery elements. However, the number of guns was increased. While the I.Abt had still had 18 10.5cm leFH 18 *Wespe*, the number of 10.5cm leFH 18 and 15cm sFH 18 was increased to six in each battery, instead of four. The s K 18 battery had four guns as before.

A *Wespe* from an unknown unit travels along a dusty track. Many crews complained of the lack of stowage space in the vehicle; here they have hung personal gear on the superstructure, including a large bag placed on the glacis plate.

The *Artillerie-Lehr-Regiment* in Jüterbog had a number of self-propelled guns for training purposes, including a number of early production versions of the *Hummel*. In the background are sheds containing a number of PzKpfw I *Fahrschulwannen* (driver training tubs).

With implementation of the PzDiv 44 and PzGrenDiv 44 the KStN were changed to the new *freie Gliederung* (free formed), a radically simplified structure initiated to save equipment.

Panzer Division 45

Facing certain defeat, the organizational structure for PzDiv 45 was developed. This was intended to serve as a basis for both PzDiv and PzGren divisions. While the combat strength of the PzRgt had been reduced to 20 PzKpfw IV and 20 PzKpfw V Panther tanks, artillery elements were not affected. The structure was not implemented on a regular basis, the remaining units continued fighting until the bitter end using whatever equipment was available.

Unit Organization

By May 1943, the *Generalstab des Heeres* published a schedule for reorganizing a number of Panzer divisions (*Heer* [army] and Waffen-SS), and also PzGrenDiv.

But the schedule could not be fulfilled in the near future. Interestingly, at end of 1943 all PzDiv and PzGrenDiv and six Waffen-SS divisions were, in the main, equipped with the planned number of self-propelled guns. Also a number of independent artillery regiments at army level were established and equipped with self-propelled guns, mainly the 15cm sFH 18 (Sfl) *Hummel*.

Three *Wespe* positioned in a snow-covered field on the Eastern Front: clearly visible is the *Rundblickfernrohr* (RblF — panoramic telescope sight) 36, a vital piece of equipment that aligned the gun with the terrain of the firing site.

8

IN COMBAT

In January 1944 the *General der Artillerie*, who was always keen to expand the reputation of his branch of the military, sent a letter to his artillery commanders outlining his views on a re-organization:

> Present day technology has had a decisive effect on our branch in the development of armour protection and mobility. Apart from the *bodenständige Artillerie* [units formed in occupied countries and equipped with captured equipment] and *Sonderartillerie* [special artillery], modern artillery can be divided in two technical and tactical groups:
>
> 1) Towed artillery [horse and motor]
> 2) Self-propelled artillery
>
> The second group will be given the designation
> *Panzerartillerie*
>
> Formed as follows:
> a) *Sturmartillerie* [assault artillery]
> b) *Selbstfahrlafette* [self-propelled] artillery
> c) Conventional Panzer artillery regiments as yet to be equipped with self-propelled guns

Directly under the control of the *General der Artillerie*, this new department was responsible for the technical advancement of the new self-propelled guns.

Evaluations of battlefield experiences sent in by self-propelled units were collected and examined in detail: The new weapon system was under steady and thorough critical observation. The German army had established a system whereby any improvements made were influenced by the information garnered

Only a small amount of ammunition was carried on a *Hummel,* but before going into battle, the vehicle would be loaded ready for action and replenished in the field by the *Munitionsstaffel* (ammunition supply team). The 15cm charges were transported in wicker containers; the shells are stacked in the back of the fighting compartment ready to be fused.

The proposal to build an advanced observer tank, based on a PzKpfw V Panther, was never realized, and this caused the *Panzerartillerie* to seek an alternative solution. A number of PzKpfw III were reconditioned and modified to carry the necessary additional radios and optical equipment: importantly the main gun assembly was removed to create more space and replaced by a dummy gun barrel. The only weapon carried was a *Maschinengewehr* (MG – machine gun) 34 mounted in the centre of the mantlet.

from combat experience reports submitted by front-line forces. These observations were collated then evaluated by the *Waffengeneräle* (branch of service departments) and a report eventually sent to the respective manufacturer where any improvements could be incorporated on production vehicles, but not every item requested could be realized. One component front-line forces constantly requested to be modified or re-designed, was the final-drive units used on the PzKpfw IV, but this would never be remedied.

However, on many occasions the combat reports were also used to question the battlefield tactics employed by front-line units.

In January 1944 a summary, using some detail extracted from combat reports, was published detailing how best to tactically deploy the self-propelled artillery. Unfortunately, the involved units were not identified, but it has been possible to identify a few units.

One unit, PzArtRgt 103, submitted a comprehensive combat experience report amounting to more than 100 pages, which describes in detail the chaotic situation on the Eastern Front.

The views expressed by the *General der Artillerie* elaborations would be instituted at the training facilities of the *Artillerieschule* (artillery school) in Jüterbog, and then filter down to field units. All lessons learned were collected and published even if they contradicted regulation tactics.

The opening paragraph of the report shows interesting observation:

By 1943, the majority of German tank units had been issued with PzKpfw IV mounting a long-barrelled 7.5cm KwK L/48, and this caused some PzArtAbt to modify their observation tanks to resemble the type. Here a PzBeobWg III from an unknown unit has been fitted with a wooden replica of the long-barrelled gun. This would have been fitted, as were the *Panzerschürzen* (side skirts) and Zimmerit anti-magnetic coating, by the field workshop units.

Reports from the Russian battlefield reveal that the self-propelled artillery units were highly effective and were, in general, considered to be the ideal support weapon for tank units.

In contrast, reports submitted from the Italian front were in general negative. The reason for this can be attributed to the difficult terrain in south and central Italy, which imposed far greater demands on the equipment. The self-propelled gun battalion could never be committed according to tactical regulations, and also because our tank force was faced with similar problems. A third reason for this negative attitude could lie in the poor equipment issued to the self-propelled battalions.

An unknown unit deployed on the *Ost* (East) front, reported its experiences with various types of *Panzerbeobachtungswagen* (PzBeobWg – observation vehicle):

The PzBeobWg (SdKfz 253) has proven reasonably successful. Disadvantages: The vehicle is much too heavy for its chassis and running gear: stub axles broke frequently. The vehicle lacks any armament and when compared to a combat tank, its cross-country mobility (trench crossing capability) is limited. The PzBeobWg III is too high, especially when accompanying the *Schützenpanzerwagen*-equipped battalion. The armament, a *Machinengewehr* [MG – machine gun] 34, is considered to be insufficient: a 2cm gun and an MG would be preferred. For a short period a PzKpfw III armed with the 5cm KwK was issued to the battery, and this gun was often used for self-defence.

We support the introduction of *Sturmgeschütz* as PzBeobWg. Advantages: A solo enemy tank which has managed to break through could be halted, thus eliminating the unappealing image of a PzBeobWg retreating from this threat and the resulting negative effect on the morale of our troops. The *Sturmgeschütz* is almost immune to anti-tank rifle fire and absorbs 3.7cm and 4.7cm hits far better than the PzBeobWg. Furthermore, the StuG is a much lower than the PzBeobWg.

Normally the forward observers worked from the PzBeobWg, but only if it could be easily concealed. In special situations the observers dismounted from the PzBeobWg with good success, allowing the tank to remain under cover. Communication was by field telephone.

This after-action report is most interesting, being one the few available describing the usage of a *leichte gepanzerter BoeobachtungsKraftwagen* (le gep BeobKw – light armoured observation vehicle), the SdKfz 253. Although designed to follow the tank regiments during an attack, the type invariably failed due to it having poor cross-country mobility. Furthermore, despite the small size of the vehicle it had a distinctive shape which the enemy easily recognized making them a preferred target. The lack of armament on observer vehicles was openly criticized, both the 250/5 and the PzBeobWg III were equipped with an MG 34, which troops deemed to be totally inadequate.

The idea of using the *Sturmgeschütz* as an observeration vehicle appears to be sensible as the armour protection and the powerful gun would give its crews it a better chance of survival.

Almost invisible on the snow-covered Russian steppe winter, the crew of a whitewashed *Wespe* awaits orders for the next fire-support mission. Six fused and ready-to-fire shells are placed on the folded down rear flap. On the left, behind the commander, is a FuSprech 'f' radio and loudspeaker.

Russia

I. Tactical experiences of self-propelled battalions on the east front:
15 August 1943, PzArtRgt 103, 4.PzDiv

The battalion (I./PzArtReg 103) was issued with two batteries of six leFH *auf Panzerfahrgestell* [tank chassis] II and one battery with six sFH *auf Panzerfahrgestell* IV. Also nine *Artillerie-Beobachtungspanzer* III and three SdKfz 250/3, [known as *Ziege* (goat) by troops], were available. On the battlefront this assemblage proved to be effective during an attack and also for defence. A combination of 10.5cm and 15cm guns, deployed in a ratio of 2:1, was more than sufficient to meet with all tactical requirements. Also it must be remembered that our Panzer divisions have more firepower available with their 7.5cm and 8.8cm guns, but ultimately all the leFH 18 should be replaced by the 15cm. However, this will not be feasible at present due to the critical situation with the supply of ammunition. Accordingly, we should strive for a perfect combination of fire from our tank weapons at a single target and the artillery to cover the area with high-explosive and shrapnel rounds.

Although the PzKpfw II chassis had proven to be mechanically unreliable when used to mount a 15cm sIG 33, due to the lack of a suitable replacement it was modified and used for the *Wespe*, but many of the original problems remained. The susceptible planetary (epicyclic) gears in the *Seitenvorglege* (final drive) units continued to fail as did the leaf springs and other parts of the running gear.

Three *Wespe* in position, two have been camouflaged with a coating of whitewash which suggests that *'Charkow'* has been recently delivered to the unit. The lack of space inside the fighting compartment has caused the crew place the ammunition behind the gun. None of the vehicles has the 2m rod antenna for the radio erected.

The most intriguing experience is the commitment of the self-propelled battalion in all combat situations; its great mobility allows the rapid establishment of firing positions while making an advance. Since the *Beobachtungs-Stellen* (observation posts) are also highly mobile, high-quality radio communication is of utmost importance.

During the fighting at Teploya, from 8 to 10 July 1943 [northern sector of Kursk], the self-propelled battalion supported the division. Our troops, despite attacking with massed formations of tanks, were unable to achieve a breakthrough. For this reason the commitment of the self-propelled guns could not take place in accord with our tactical plan. As a result the advantages of the self-propelled battalion could not be used to full effect.

However, the advantages of the self-propelled guns were decisive in the armoured battles in the east:

1. While the conventional towed gun batteries had numerous casualties due to frequent enemy air raids and artillery fire, the self-propelled guns, relying on their armour protection, were able to simply leave their fire positions – even under heavy fire. This was all the more important, since the self-propelled guns were often forced to move into exposed positions.

2. During a critical situation, when the enemy launched a counterattack supported by artillery, only the armoured self-propelled gun battalion was able to carry on the firefight.

3. Defensively, the self-propelled artillery enabled a mobile and often surprising commitment. An amazing sight was the advance by 18 self-propelled guns, in side-by-side formation, into a newly selected firing position. The massive concentration of fire that followed was impressive and proved to be most successful. After each mission the battalion could securely leave the position before the enemy could respond.

The condition of the many unmade roads in Russia during the *Rasputitsa* (mud season), slowed the German advance. Here a *Hummel* from PzArtRgt 102 of 9.PzDiv has slid off the roadway and become bogged-down and awaits recovery: note the heavy towing bar positioned under the gun. Invariably this type of incident would result in damage to the vulnerable running gear.

4. The self-propelled guns were also able to defend against enemy armour attempting to break through our lines during the back and forth flow of many battles in the east. At Znamenskoye, 50km northeast of Orel, No.4 battery had repelled eight tanks attacking from the right flank: after spotting the enemy approaching over open terrain, the self-propelled guns were manoeuvred to face the threat before opening fire at 1,500m range using hollow-charge rounds fitted with impact fuses. The rapid fire encouraged the enemy tanks to retreat.

5. The self-propelled guns must never be committed in anything other than battalion strength. If our tank assault gets stopped, a single self-propelled gun battery is no help. As a result, the battalion must always use the concentrated fire from all of its 18 guns to destroy enemy forces. It is important to avoid long stops during action as this would give the enemy time to attack. Targets for the self-propelled artillery are not a single weapon, but trench systems, fortified towns, anti-tank gun nests, stretches of woodland and gun positions concealed in a valley or behind a slope.

6. After breaking through the enemy lines our tank assault will achieve a speed conventional artillery cannot reliably follow, and also it takes up precious time to attach or detach the guns from their towing vehicles, whereas the self-propelled battalion is able to follow closely. When a tank attack will becomes stalled, our self-propelled artillery guns can immediately be brought in to action to assist. When the tanks will continue on their assault, the self-propelled battalion will follow.

PzArtRgt 103 had been established with a full complement of self-propelled guns in accordance to the KStN structures. But, instead of being issued with five le BeobPzWg (SdKfz 250/5), it received three *leichte Funkpanzerwagen*

The crew of this *Wespe* has thoroughly concealed its vehicle with foliage, but has chosen a poor location. During action the gun has sunk into the soft ground and will have to be hauled out by a recovery team. Any attempt to drive out could cause terminal damage to the ever-delicate final-drive units.

(le FuPzWg – light armoured radio vehicle – SdKfz 250/3). Standard tactical practice stated that during an offensive, after successful breakthrough the tank regiment would then continue to make a rapid advance. However in 1943 this was no longer valid when faced by an enemy with a superior amount of armour and which had begun to adopt the once-successful German tactics.

The decision to commit the self-propelled guns only in battalion strength is understandable, but not always possible on the battlefield. Also the vehicles were vulnerable, any that had a mechanical failure or battle damage had to be withdrawn; replacement was not a simple matter.

The *Wespe* and *Hummel* were sufficiently armoured to protect the crew against small arms fire and shrapnel.

Report on PzArtRgt 103´s tactical possibilities when faced with shortages of personnel and equipment

I.) Regimental staff battery
Due to the loss of six important signals vehicles the strength of the telephone echelon has decreased to 30 percent; that of the radio echelon to 60 percent. This led to a situation where both personnel and equipment became overburdened.

II.) I./PzArtRgt 103

III.) II./PzArtRgt 103

A PzBeobWg III from
2.SS-PzDiv Das Reich:
The *Sternantenne* (star
antenna) mounted on
the engine deck was
used for long-range
communications (Fu 8
radio). The vehicle has been
fitted with *Panzerschürzen*
(side skirts) by field
engineers; note the flimsy
mounting brackets. The
crew is wearing the 1943-
type two-piece combat
uniform, with a distinctive
camouflage pattern, issued
to Waffen-SS units.

The SdKfz 250/5
*leichte gepanzerter
Beobachtungwagen* (le gep
BeobKw – light armoured
observation vehicle) was
known to the troops as
the *Beobachter-Ziege*
(observer's goat). Note
the *Maschinengewehr*
(MG – machine gun) 42
held in position by straps
attached to brackets inside
the vehicle.

Gun situation

A total of 11 of the 12 leFH 18 (Sfl) *Wespe*, and three of six sFH 18 *Hummel* (with one returning soon from the workshop) are ready for combat.

Armoured Observation Vehicles

Instead of 12 armoured observation posts and forward observers (including battalion command post), only five can be made operational to support the remaining observation vehicles (42 percent).

Vehicles

Forward observers cannot be motorized due to the lack of vehicles – each battery only had one instead of nine. This lack of light passenger cars made the transmission of information between mobile leadership and command difficult, if not impossible.

Transport of Ammunition

For the eleven *Wespe* only 730 rounds, instead of the authorized 1,386 can be transported; for the four *Hummel* only 120 rounds instead of 264. This means that the 15 guns of the battalion cannot be used concentrated on focal points.

Truck Situation

The poor mechanical state of most of our trucks has forced us to use the ammunition trucks for other purposes; endangering the supply to our guns. The workshop has only two mechanically reliable trucks instead of ten.

All PzBeobWg III were produced by utilizing redundant PzKpfw III tanks which in the first instance were returned to the factory for a complete overhaul, which resulted in a non-standardized vehicle. For instance there were five different versions of the extra armour fitted to the glacis plate. The first vehicles delivered to front-line forces were not fitted with *Panzerschürzen* (side skirts); these would be fitted in the field as they became availabile.

VI.) Conclusion

Due to the above mentioned numbers, the performance of the regiment has decreased by approximately 50 percent. The regiment could fulfill all assigned tasks, but this was possible only by sacrificing the remaining vehicles and completely overburdening the soldiers. The regiment has been permanently in combat since 22 June 1941. It seems necessary to rest and re-equip the unit at a training garrison.

In 1944, a number of improvements were designed for the *Hummel* and included modified air intakes to prevent dust entering the engine compartment. Also the compartment for the driver was significantly widened.

The situation for I.Abt and II.Abt, both armed with towed guns, was similar. By the end of 1943, the ever-present shortages became even more critical endangering the health and fighting capabilities of front-line German units.

The unit submitted more detailed technical reports:

Technical experience report on the *Hummel* and *Wespe* self-propelled guns and the PzBeobWg III:

1) The *Hummel* built utilizing components from the PzKpfw III/IV did not prove to be reliable in operation. The use of unskilled drivers can be blamed to a lesser extent. However, it became clear that the chassis is severely overloaded by the heavy 15cm sFH 18. In detail the following deficiencies arose:

Any breakages of the teeth on a final-drive sprocket will usually destroy the complete final-drive unit.

During combat frequent side-to-side steering movements while stationary overloaded the cover bolts on the final drive units resulting in them shearing off.

The bearing and bearing housing for the idler wheel broke quite frequently. This was partly caused by there not being an overload link in the track.

Problems with the engine cooling and cooler leakages did not occur frequently. We advise that a cover plate should be fitted over the exhaust muffler to deflect bullets and shrapnel.

2) So far the PzKpfw II chassis on the *Wespe* has only suffered excessive wear to the teeth of the idler wheel and its trunnions. Also, there is a tendency for oil to contaminate the brakes.

3) The Variorex transmission on the PzBeobWg III has the same serious problems as experienced with the *Hummel*. Apparently these tanks were repaired using salvaged components. That became noticeable when a chassis number had to be quoted when ordering spare parts; in many cases the parts did not fit. After changing an engine we frequently noticed that the transmission and the final-drive units often failed. Suspension torsion bars also failed with some frequency. We lost only one PzBeobWg III to enemy action, when the rear armour near the air inlet was penetrated.

Despite the most intensive efforts by the workshop team, some 66 percent of our PzBeobWg were continuously unserviceable.

PzArtRgt 76 of 6.PzDiv was issued with *Wespe* self-propelled guns at the beginning of September 1943, and on 16 October submitted their first combat experience report:

A complete battery of 15cm sFH 18 auf Gw IV *Hummel* in firing position: The wide plains of Russia were ideal for tank deployments, the terrain being firm and the openness allowed wide turns to be made which did not overload final-drive units.

Above: The crew of this *Hummel* has used bundles straw to disguise the outline of their vehicle. Camouflage was important: by 1944, the Soviet air force had gained control of the skies over the battlefield. Note that at the rear a mud flap was fitted on early production vehicles to reduce the dust cloud created during marches. The vehicle carries a non-standard *Balkenkreuz*.

A 15cm sIG 33 *Grille* auf Gw 38(t) Ausf H, possibly from 26.PzDiv, positioned in the remains of a power sub-station in Italy. To the right a second *Grille* has been camouflaged under a pile of wooden planks and an SdKfz 251/1 of the platoon headquarters has been carefully parked near to the building out of sight of patrolling Allied aircraft.

Mobility on the march:

The speed of a *Wespe* battery on the march is much slower when compared to a motorized battalion. The conditions on the Russian battlefield mean that we cannot go faster than 18 to 20kph. During longer marches it is advisable to separate the tracked from the wheeled vehicles. Marches over longer distances inevitably resulted in a considerable number of mechanical failures, many due to the engines not being correctly run-in, and also the lack of experienced drivers.

The dire transport situation complicated the delivery of fuel. While the fuel consumption of the battery has greatly increased after conversion to self-propelled guns (six *Wespe* and two *Munitionsträger*), we still have only one truck to transport fuel. The long distances we have to march forced us to send the fuel truck back two or three times to keep the battery fuelled.

During a transfer on 2 October 1943 (Tshigerin - Omelnik) only *Flieger-Brennstoff* [aviation fuel] was available. The engines were not adjusted to use this type of fuel and overheated damaging pipes and joints in the cooling system. The aviation fuel also made the supply pipes brittle and they easily failed; spare pipes were not available. One *Wespe* had to run on only one fuel tank. Due to the fuel transport problems, the battery was dependent on the services of the PzRgt.

The training situation

Instruction and training on the *Wespe* began on 6 September 1943. The three-man crew was trained on all aspects of the gun; the commander was also trained to use

A PzBeobWg III of 1.SS-PzDiv Leibstandarte Adolf Hitler (LAH) passes through a Russian village. Parts of the *Panzerschürzen* (side skirts) have been ripped off their flimsy mounting brackets. The improved frontal armour has proved to be of value; a hit on the front plate, near the left-hand towing bracket, has not made a penetration.

radio equipment [previously this was by telephone or flag signals]. In general, 14 days is sufficient for our men to be become fully acquainted with the new self-propelled guns.

The training of the drivers remains inadequate. This became apparent, when training had to be halted when we were forced to retreat. Following three days of rain, which turned the terrain into a quagmire, many drivers were not able assess the performance of the vehicles. Engines tended to overheat: in one *Wespe* a piston got stuck by the heat, one ran out of fuel due to a pump failure and another slid off the road breaking the final-drive units. The battery did not have a recovery trailer and all the nearest repair workshop facilities were busy which forced us to tow the *Wespe*, on its running wheels, for 200km. Consequently, the rubber-tyres on the wheels were badly damaged and many leaf springs failed.

By pure coincidence it was found that the ammunition stowed in the left-hand front bin became too hot to be handled. As a result for all marches longer than 30km, the ammunition has to be taken out and carried elsewhere.

Further problems and modifications

On one occasion the fire extinguisher went off unassisted. The transport cradle for the *Rundblickfernrohr* (RblF – panoramic periscope sight) was relocated at the request of the K1 (gunner). Extra brackets were fitted to carry a spare barrel for the MG, gas masks and a spare stadia rod for the gun. Strong brackets must be mounted on the front plate of the superstructure to carry spare road wheels. The intercom system is very unreliable and fails frequently due to condensers burning out; spare parts are rarely available.

A column of *Hummel* self-propelled guns from 1.SS-PzDiv LAH pass supply vehicles of the PzArtAbt: In order to protect the gun and mounting, the barrel was lowered onto the travel rest. But as it was not possible to release it from inside the fighting compartment in an emergency situation, many units fabricated their own solution.

The *Wespe* carries one *Maschinengewehr* and two *Maschinenpistole*, the commander carries a pistol. Any attempt to carry further weapons is not advisable due to the lack of free space, also no carrying brackets are fitted.

The demolition charge [for self-destruction] should be fitted between the rear ammunition bins. Four ammunition drums (MG) can be stowed adjacent to the left of the gun barrel, one ammunition drum (MG) can be stowed under the barrel, and another under the inertia-starter unit. The position of the starter and the gun traverse gear prevents any further stowage.

The towing ropes supplied with each *Wespe* are too thin and not sufficiently strong to haul the gun. On several occasion these ropes broke after few kilometers.

The *Wespe* must never be used for towing other self-propelled guns.

During the *Schlammperiode* [mud season] only half-track tractors proved to be suited to supply the battery with ammunition, food and fuel.

A further after-action report describes details of the tactical commitment of a self-propelled gun battalion.

US Army troops inspect a *Hummel* and a SdKfz 251/1 from 1./PzArtRgt Das Reich (DR) which have been abandoned in a French village after the D-Day landings on 6 June 1944. The *Hummel* carries the name 'Clausewitz' to indicate that it is 'C' gun in the battery.

An early production *Hummel*, from an unidentified unit, has been worked on by engineers at a field workshop. The travel rest has been modified to allow a quick release of the barrel; the two Bosch headlamps are fitted with simple but effective guards. A steel plate has been welded to the front of the recuperator as a protection against small arms fire.

7 December 1943 [unspecified unit]

Tactically, the battalion works exclusively with the *gepanzerte Stosstruppe* [armoured assault force]: the Panzer regiment, the armoured rifle regiment, the armoured engineers or the *Sturmgeschütze*. The battalion was under the orders of the commander of the PzRgt. This method was well-proven, since the battalion was only faced with missions it was able to accomplish. If attached to an *ungepanzerte* [unarmoured] unit, which lacked knowledge of our weaknesses and strengths, the self-propelled battalion would be at risk of being used as *Sturmgeschütz* or a break-through unit.

The prime objective of a self-propelled battalion is to suppress the Soviet *PaK-Fronten* (anti-tank gun lines) during advance or retreat of our tank formations. Forward positions must be prepared, or quickly chosen when closely following the advance of the tanks. Soon after a breakthrough, Soviet troops will attempt to close their lines again. Then the self-propelled battalion must keep close to the PzRgt in order not to become involved in any skirmishing with enemy infantry. It is worth noting that the self-propelled guns are immune to infantry fire, but are vulnerable to armour-piercing ammunition. Repeatedly, such attacks were easily defeated by the battalion, but this was not their prime mission. Normally the batteries will form a Batterie-Nest [dug-in gun position]. The heavy battery will be closely flanked by the two light batteries, guarding to both sides in a curved line. Often one gun will be positioned at the rear to defend tanks attacking from this direction. This hedgehog-shaped position proved to be ideal for attacking advancing enemy infantry or tanks.

The proposal for the battery commanders and the VBs, to alternate their movements during the advance – one directs fire from a prominent position while the other is on the move – is wishful thinking and proved to be impractical. To achieve this we would

A group of *vorgeschobener-Beobachter* (VB – forward observer), in an SdKfz 250/5 observation vehicle receive orders from a 4.PzDiv officer. Note the armoured-steel cover protecting the susceptible porcelain insulator for the antenna mounting.

Frequent replenishment with fuel, ammunition and food was essential for all front-line units. Here a *Wespe*, from an unidentified unit, has fuel from a 200-litre drum pumped into the two fuel tanks positioned under the floor at the rear of the fighting compartment.

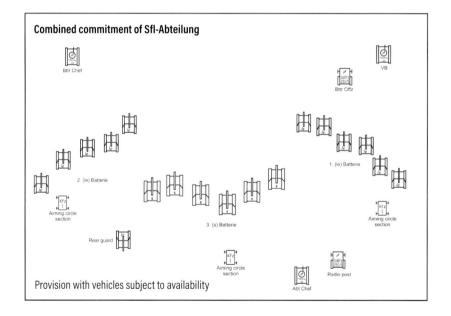

Combined commitment of Sfl-Abteilung

Bttr Chef

VB

Bttr Offz

1. (le) Batterie

2. (le) Batterie

Aiming circle section

Aiming circle section

3. (s) Batterie

Rear guard

Aiming circle section

Radio post

Abt Chef

Provision with vehicles subject to availability

need double the number of PzBeobWg and be aware that some 50 percent would not be combat ready due to constant mechanical damages. Furthermore, we consider that this approach would lead to an unacceptable loss of personnel.

Another report further explains the tactics employed by a Panzer artillery battery equipped with self-propelled guns. The mechanical unreliability of the

PzBeobWg III is referred to once again, and would be repeatedly commented on until the war ended:

15 December 1943 [unspecified unit]

Since being re-established and re-equipped [with self-propelled guns gun], the battalion has been used only in the defensive role. Tactically it was deployed in the same way as a towed artillery battalion. New radio equipment has not been delivered, so we still have the same radios as the towed artillery.
The following experiences were encountered:

1. Choice of the firing position.
This is now a simple task due to the mobility of the self-propelled gun. The universal principle of 'a free line of sight to spot enemy tanks is more important than camouflage' no longer applies. To avoid losses due to enemy tank attacks the battery must not remain in a side-by-side formation, but will have to disperse in order not to present an easy target. Also in this way our considerable anti-tank capabilities will be deployed over the entire front. The following establishment proved correct: With enemy tanks attacking, two or three self-propelled guns remained in the firing position as long as the forward observer or the close observation post was able to operate. The other guns moved out to the right and left-hand side of this position as they need an unobstructed free line of fire. The advantage of this type of weapon is that when concealed in a firing position it

Five 15cm sFH 18 auf Gw IV *Hummel* self-propelled guns from three batteries that formed s HArtAbt 843 which operated as an independent army troop unit and was deployed at points of main effort as *Sturmgeschütz*.

can fulfill an artillery-style fire mission without being harmed by enemy tanks. If all the observation posts are lost due to the tactical situation, these guns will also be used to defend against enemy tanks.

On 10 November 1943, due to this type of deployment a Russian counterattack by tanks and infantry was repelled. No.1 battery achieved 18 confirmed and four unconfirmed kills, No.2 battery confirmed three and No.3 battery confirmed nine kills. The action took place over a 5-hour period during which the battalion suffered no losses.

2. Keeping close the lines of our infantry

Both the *Wespe* and *Hummel* are very mobile and have armour sufficient to protect the crew from rifle fire and shrapnel. This allows both types to approach closer to enemy infantry positions. Although it is more difficult to find cover for these guns, due to their greater height when compared to a towed gun, it is considered to be a minor disadvantage. The many advantages of getting closer to enemy infantry positions are as follows:

- Shorter wire for telephone connection to the observation post.
- Better radio communication to the forward observer.
- A saving of material by firing smaller charges.
- Quicker to defend against enemy breakthroughs or a possible counterattack.
- A positive effect on the morale of our infantry. This was repeatedly observed whenever our thin infantry lines needed support. Under such conditions the search for alternative firing positions becomes more important.

After every change of position the guns had to be re-sighted, which is very quick to achieve. The driver has a rudimentary sighting device, which makes the adjustment of the gun much easier.

The defensive success of the self-propelled guns with their very limited anti-tank capacities is remarkable. However in 1943, Soviet tank commanders had improved their tactical skills but their cooperation with their infantry and artillery remained somewhat limited.

A report from an unidentified self-propelled battalion records some of their experiences:

31 December 1943

When the battalion is committed within the range of an armoured group the tasks for both have been clearly evaluated and determined. If an attack against a difficult target is ordered, the complete battalion will accompany the advance. The battalion commander and battery commanders in PzBeobWg (armoured observation vehicles) will be in close contact with the battlegroup leader who will open fire the instant a target emerges. After accomplishing this task the self-propelled battalion will then follow the battlegroup.

The batteries need better protection for their vehicles. For this reason a number of PzGren in armoured halftracks are to be attached to defend the guns against marauding infantry, allowing the crews to concentrate on their artillery mission. The request comes after losing two *Hummel* to Soviet infantrymen who tossed hand grenades into each vehicle. Concentrated fire from the entire battalion was nearly always successful.

Although the most important advantage for the self-propelled artillery is its great mobility, armour protection for the crew is equally important. When on mobile defensive duty, the guns were used for days in terrain interspersed with enemy infantry positions; it was here where this protection against small arms fire became vitally important.

Other experiences:

On 31 August 1943, due to the tactical situation our batteries were forced to fire from concealed positions behind our frontline. At 17:00hrs a Russian radio message was intercepted, urging their forces to annihilate the battalion. Around 10 minutes later a heavy barrage hit our firing positions, which we had successfully abandoned. No losses were reported.

On 26 September 1943 at 05:00hrs, the Russians set up positions in battalion strength at the gates of Ljubetsh. No.2 battery moved into open firing positions and began firing at

In January 1945, *Festung* (Fortress) Budapest was surrounded by the Red Army. A *Hummel* has been moved into the city and thoroughly camouflaged with foliage to conceal it from marauding enemy aircraft. The gun is possibly in service with 13.PzDiv as what remained of the unit was left to defend the city.

Three le gep BeobKw (SdKfz 250/5) from PzArtRgt 93 in 26.PzDiv: The unit was in France from October 1942 until it was transferred to Italy in 1943, under the command of *Oberstleutnant* Johann Rizicka, where it was to remain until the war in Europe ended at 02:41hrs on 7 May 1945.

short range (200 to 300m) targeting their entrenched infantry. The Russians were repelled with considerable losses, forcing the battalion to retreat. We had only one injured.

On 28 October 1943, unexpected fire from a Russian 17.2cm battery hit our firing positions. Thanks to the armour protection on our self-propelled guns, the battalion lost neither personnel nor material.

Italian Front

The experiences made in the Italian theatre of war were totally different from those being reported by units deployed in Russia.

In November 1943, the *Waffenamt* reported after an informative tour of front-line units in Italy:

> Experiences with self-propelled artillery guns (*Wespe* and *Hummel*)
> The objective was to get a clear view of the combat experiences with *Wespe* and *Hummel* in the Italian theatre of war and to establish a close contact with these units. For this an officer from the WaA (*Hauptmann* Maas) accompanied by an officer from *Artillerie-Schule* II (*Oberleutnant* Prinz von Hohenlohe) were sent to Italy. During the period 16 to 26 September 1943 the following units of XIV Panzer-Korps were visited:
> 15.PzGrenDiv

PzDiv Hermann Göring
3.PzGrenDiv
26.PzDiv

Additional units were met while travelling:
16. Pzdiv
29. PzDiv
PzDiv SS Leibstandarte Adolf Hitler

The journey to the front was an urgent necessity because Sfl units fighting on the Italian front have submitted a number of very negative and critical reports. These contradict the many reports received from units fighting on the Eastern Front.

The main difference between the fighting in Russia and Italy is the terrain, which in both the south and mid-Italy is mountainous. The many narrow passes, steep ascents, tight curves and a hard, rocky ground are unsuitable for the passage of heavy tracked vehicles. Consequently our vehicles suffered more failures when compared to our vehicles operating over the more level terrain in Russia. Another factor is that the summer temperatures this year in Italy have been very high.

The terrain and the tactics employed by the enemy controlled how the battle was conducted. Our planned commitment of using self-propelled guns to provide close-support fire to a Panzer division could not be performed in Italy. In most instances the self-propelled guns were used in platoon strength or as solo gun. Thus only few experiences in regard to the tactical commitment of the self-propelled guns could be made.

The combat troops presented the following experiences:

1) The Maybach engines in the *Wespe* and *Hummel* lack sufficient power, which make the guns far too slow and only manage 33 percent of the normal road speed of a towed (motorized) battalion. A march by the complete battery is not possible due to the constant mechanical failures. All the guns have to be moved individually.

2) Performing tight turns around the many bends in the mountains frequently caused the final-drive units on the *Wespe* to break. The running gear on the *Hummel* caused many problems due to transverse joints breaking.

3) Both types had serious problems with their brakes, the brake bands overheated and wore out and the retaining bolts sheared. During a 320km march 26.PzDiv consumed the entire stock of brake bands and spare running wheels. However, the march did take place in the extreme heat of August.

4) The inventories of spare parts were generally insufficient, and self-propelled gun battalion in 3.PzGrenDiv had no workshop facilities available.

5) Both 26.PzDiv and 3.PzGrenDiv reported that the PzBeobWg built on PzKpfw III had been fitted with old engines, which failed frequently. Also some of the welded seams on parts of the *Wespe* had been carelessly executed and were opening.

Due to these shortcomings, 3.PzGrenDiv had only 11 out of 18 *Wespe* operational, despite the guns having been delivered just a few weeks earlier.

After four weeks of combat, 26.PzDiv reported two out of 12 *Wespe* and one out of six *Hummel* as operational. When the unit withdrew from the frontline, four *Hummel*, three *Wespe* and five PzBeobWg had to be blown up by their crews after suffering minor mechanical damage. This is extremely worrying, because during this period only two guns had been destroyed by the enemy.

Both leFH 18 and sFH 18 (towed and self-propelled) suffered from the recuperator and gun cradle not being protected with armour. All divisions reported repeated damage to these components by shrapnel and rifle fire.

The lack of space for the crews, especially in the *Wespe*, was a continuous problem. Other than the gun crew and ammunition, there was little space left for their personal gear (blankets, bags, haversacks and canteen).

Observation vehicles and wireless equipment

It was reported by 3.PzGrenDiv that they lacked sufficient radios, they did not have a PzBeobWg, and had only one 30W radio for each battery. The 30W radios could only be used for contact between the battery and higher echelons, but not for fire direction as intended. This is all the more troublesome, because these were the most reliable radios available.

The 26.PzDiv had transferred their remaining PzBeobWg (PzKpfw III) to rear areas since the type could not cope with the Italian terrain. The SdKfz 250/1 armoured halftracks they used instead for observation proposes had very good mobility and wireless equipment.

By evaluating their previous experiences the troop has indentified a number of requirements regarding self-propelled guns:

1) Easier way to dismount the gun for exchange or repair to save as much time as possible.
2) The side traverse must be increased; ideally 360° for all-round fire.
3) Each battalion must be provided with more men for the maintenance section or be issued with a workshop platoon.
4) Radio telephony

The PzBeobWg must be provided with a 30W and a 10W radio [Fu 8 and Fu 5], or an improved FuSprech 'f'. It is most desirable to have an increased allotment of FuSprech 'g'.

Despite having numerous flaws the self-propelled guns, especially the *Wespe*, have proven invaluable in the east, but the current versions are not suitable for combat in the mountains of Italy.

All PzArt regiments issued with self-propelled guns for combat in Italy would prefer to be issued with towed motorized battalions. As a result, the guns should only be used in combat when accompanied by tanks.

In general it is recognized by corps, divisional and also regimental staffs that the artillery is an important element for a defensive battle. During interrogation many British and American prisoners have mentioned the power of our artillery and how much it is feared.

On 1 September 1943, the *höherer PanzerOffizier* (hPzOffz – senior armour officer) at the *Oberkommando Süd* (OB – commander in chief south) reported:

Experiences with leFH (*Wespe*)

During a visit by the senior PzOffz to the attached divisions it was found that, according consistent complaints by the troop, the LeFH (*Wespe*) is not suitable for use in the mountainous terrain of the Italian theatre.

Many losses of the type have been indentified as being caused by mechanical problems:
1) The chassis of the *Wespe* proved to be too weak for the strains of travelling and live-fire missions. Consequently the engine, the transmission and the springs of the running wheels are subjected to heavy wear.
2) The resulting failures cannot be covered due to the poor situation with the supply of spare parts.

The powerful recoil of the 15cm gun has pressed the running gear on this *Hummel* deep into the mud. This is an early production vehicle identifiable by the large exhaust muffler mounted on the rear plate, but as fumes from the exhaust easily entered the fighting compartment it was soon removed from production vehicles.

A total of seven PzBeobWg III and two SdKfz 250/5 formed the staff section of PzArtRgt 93 in 26.PzDiv. First established in France during October 1942, the unit was transferred to Italy in August 1943 where it served until the end of the war.

More than 150
Munitionspanzer
(ammunition carriers)
were built on the Gw II
chassis. The 10.5cm leFH 18
was not installed; and the
embrasure covered by a
steel plate. It required little
effort to mount the gun
from a damaged *Wespe*
in the vehicle to retain the
firepower of a unit.

3) The workshop platoons have not been able to reduce the serious backlog of work.

4) There is a lack of recovery services for when the unit is moved to different locations. The speed of the self-propelled gun is significantly lower than that of our tanks. When on the advance the type cannot keep pace with other forces, during the retreat the self-propelled guns must be ordered to leave first to avoid them being destroyed or captured by advancing enemy forces. The training of drivers continues to be insufficient and the lack of experienced mechanics in the workshop only makes the situation even worse. As a result, many vehicles which normally would have survived had to be abandoned or blown up. For these reasons the disadvantages of the type clearly outweigh any benefits. The division would welcome the *Wespe* battalion being converted to a mot-Zug (motor traction) battalion.

II.

To avoid losses among the tracked vehicles the divisions requests the following:

1) When issued with new armoured vehicles they should be supported by specially-equipped workshop platoons. Thus any damage or mechanical repairs can be made properly and efficiently.

2) The training of drivers and *Panzerwarte* (armoured maintenance men) for tracked vehicles should be amalgamated in special facilities in Germany. However, these training units are unable to match demand due to the shortage of training vehicles, fuel and suitably experienced instructors.

3) The dedicated *Bergezüge* (recovery platoons) must be issued with the required equipment to enable the rapid recovery of damaged tracked vehicles after a battle.

Part of the production PzKpfw III/IV chassis was also diverted to produce *Munitionspanzer* (ammunition carrier). A thoroughly whitewashed *Munitionspanzer* passes a column of supply vehicles in April 1944 and despite the fact that it is a carrier the vehicle has a gun travel rest.

The mountainous terrain in Italy proved to be a most difficult challenge for the German forces as every type of tracked vehicle was susceptible to mechanical damage. Every failed vehicle would tie up a lot of workshop and recovery services capacity. All of this severely affected the readiness of numerous German units, leaving many with only a fraction of the combat-ready vehicles they required to continue fighting.

Radio Problems

In January 1944, the *Waffenamt* published a compilation of experience reports detailing the many problems with the radio equipment issued to the PzArtAbt (self-propelled gun battalion).

The radio network of the artillery regiment depended on medium-wave radio equipment, while that of a Panzer regiment on FM equipment. Originally communications between the two was only possible for higher echelons. This is barely comprehensible and can be regarded as a fatal error made by military planners. The report continues:

> 27 June 1943
>
> a) The 30W *Mittelwellen Gerät* (MW – medium-wave radio) was used for communication between the battery commander and the firing positions, and also between the battalion commander and the battery commanders. The equipment has proved effective. The problem exists when contacting another waveband where the radios needed careful and precise tuning. The FM radios can be simply switched between preset frequencies.
>
> b) The FuSprech 'f' used for contact between the battery officer and each gun worked outstandingly.
>
> c) The intercom system on the self-propelled gun did not work well and often failed; the reason could not always be determined. In the case of the PzBeobWg III – this could be caused by the failure of a single component being damaged due to shocks or vibrations – all communication between the commander and his driver would be lost. A sufficient amount of replacement components must be retained to allow a rapid repair.
> The driver of a *Hummel* or *Wespe* is isolated from his commander and any disruption to communications could have fatal consequences. To overcome a failure, a simple 'in the field' modification was made; a series of lights was installed for the driver:
>
> | | |
> |---|---|
> | White | Turn left |
> | Green | Start or accelerate |
> | Red | Slow down or halt |
> | Blue | Turn right |

d) The radio connection between the artillery regiment and the tank regiment is spasmodic. The tanks are fitted with FM radios and the artillery elements have MW radios, making direct contact impossible. We installed 10W FM radios in both observation vehicles in the battalion and this improved the situation almost instantly.

This is supported by a report from another unknown unit:

15 July 1942

Radio connection

Recent combat has shown that the double enciphering of radio messages required by the division led to serious time delays. Telephone connections, by no means the modern way to communicate, had to be frequently used. During a large-scale operation the telephone wire was soon destroyed by tank tracks and shell bursts. The battalion has used up half its stock of cable during the last days of combat.

The order to double encipher must be dropped.

The 30W radio has proven reliable for day and night service; not one battery lost connection. The FuSprechGer 'f' did not prove as useful since it was too easily damaged. We request the installation of 10W FM radios in each observation tank and each self-propelled gun.

There was no uniform method or order given to front-line units as to how to apply camouflage paint. In February 1943, most German tanks and other armour being delivered were painted in dark yellow; the choice of camouflage scheme was left to an individual front-line unit. Here a *Hummel* has been camouflaged with wavy bands of olive green and dark brown painted over the basic dark yellow.

An NCO from SS-PzArtRgt 5 in 5.SS-PzDiv Wiking, in conversation with the driver of an early production *Hummel*: The only defensive weaponry mounted on the vehicle was a *Maschinengewehr* (MG — machine gun) 34 for close-defence, while the crew was equipped with two *Maschinenpistole* (MP — machine pistol) 40.

Further comments by another unknown unit:

3 November 1943

a) Radio connection

During the recent mobile fighting all communications, including combat reports and fire commands were transmitted by radio only. Telephone connections would be instantly destroyed when the fighting began. The available radio equipment proved to be sufficient and the 30W medium-wave radios worked well. We request that the FuSprechGer 'f', which too easily damaged, is replaced by a 10W FM radio. The battalion did not use the FuSprechGer 'f' in our PzBeobWg III. The FuSprechGer 'g' worked very well, but only in the daytime, after dark its range decreased significantly.

b) Intercom

The intercom fitted in the self-propelled guns and PzBeobWg III were too unreliable and of little use in combat. After replacing the 2A fuses in the *Panzerkasten* (connecting box) 23 with 3A fuses, these malfunctions were mainly remedied.

c) Enciphering

We noticed that the double enciphering is too time consuming. For this reason, target points in fire missions were transmitted in clear language.

Another report dated 13 November 1943:

> Wireless connection
> Due to many problems with the radios, a secure command connection to the batteries was always at risk. As a stand-by measure we installed an additional speaking tube to connect the gun commander to the driver.

The list of experience reports dealing with radio equipment is extensive and virtually all contain similar problems, especially in case of the FuSprechGer 'f' radio and the intercom systems where they concur on the most common faults.

In early 1944, the *General der Artillerie* published an article explaining his suggestions for a series of improvements to the *Hummel*, many of which could be carried out at field workshops. To improve communication between commander and driver, he suggests the fitting of a simple speaking tube. Reports from a number units indicated that this modification was of help.

Self-propelled Artillery on French Chassis

In May 1943 the fighting in North Africa, where a number of German units had been annihilated, was reaching a bitter end, military planners decided to re-establish one of those lost units: 21.PzDiv. An extreme shortage of equipment forced the division to equip PzRgt 100 primarily with *Beutegerät* (captured equipment). These were refurbished French tanks, mainly Renault-built PzKpfw R-39(f) and Somua-built PzKpfw S-35(f) which were outclassed by 1943 standards and also lacked vital spare parts: In January 1944, it was

Three *Wespe* from SS-PzArtRgt 5 in ready-to-fire position: The fighting compartment on the type was cramped; beside the three-man crew and other equipment, room had to found to stow some 30 rounds and charges of 10.5cm ammunition. The lack of a recoil spade frequently resulted in damage to the running gear.

Two *Wespe* in position to provide support fire during the battle on the Kursk salient; both vehicles have been camouflaged against being spotted by patrolling Ilyushin Il-2 Shturmovik ground-attack aircraft (known as the 'Flying Tank') of the Soviet air force. The crew of the nearest gun has mounted the MG 34 and fitted it with a *Fliegervisier* (anti-aircraft gun sight). Note the 2m rod antenna has been erected to allow radio communictions.

reported that all PzKpfw S-35(f) were unserviceable due to the lack of clutches.

On 10 June 1944, PzRgt 100 received German equipment with the delivery of 112 PzKpfw IV and a reported 33 self-propelled guns built on French chassis.

The PzArtRgt was supplied with 22 Lorraine *Panzerhaubitze* mounting a 10.5cm leFH 18, and also 11 Lorraine mounting a 15cm sFH 13. A further 13 Lorraine were delivered to serve as armoured observation vehicles. The 21.PzDiv had an integral assault gun battalion, but it was not equipped with assault guns. Instead, it was equipped with 12 Hotchkiss-built H-39 mounting a 7.5cm PaK 40, and also 24 Hotchkiss H-39 mounting a 10.5cm leFH 16 or a 15cm leFH 18. PzArtRgt 155 was equipped with self-propelled guns built using a French-built tank chassis.

From October 1944, the unit began to receive a growing number of German-built types including StuG and PzKpfw IV. The process of rearming would take time.

In January 1944, the *General der Artillerie* (GenArt) reported:

21.PzDiv
1) Demonstration of leFH and sFH [13] built on French chassis during live firing trials have shown that leFH is more stable than when mounted in a *Wespe*. The sFH has a range of

up to 6,400m, and is therefore not suitable as artillery. Is it possible to substitute it with 12 *Hummel* self-propelled guns? The remaining sFH 13 could be given to the PzGrenRgt.

2) The StuG battalion in the division is an insufficiently armoured self-propelled gun battalion only. We ask whether a rearming to assault guns is possible, or whether a renaming should be executed.

3) The division is issued with small French tracked vehicles serving as PzBeobWg observation vehicles. These are small, inconspicuous and most agile, but only weakly armoured. Is their substitution by PzBeobwg of German origin possible?

These questions show that the GenArt doubted the mechanical reliability and combat value of the ex-French material. It is interesting to note that the 10.5cm leFH 18/1 auf Gw Lorraine scored well in direct comparison to a *Wespe*, mainly due to the type being extremely stable when firing as it was fitted with a recoil rear spade; these were never used on German self-propelled guns.

Combat Losses

The surviving war diary of the GenArt contains only few strength reports. A compilation of these was published on 1 October 1944, and they reveal a number of surprising changes.

In principle, the self-propelled gun provided far better mobility than conventional towed artillery, since the fully-tracked vehicles could be moved quickly and brought to readiness in very short time. The radio-equipped guns allowed commanders to utilize the true flexibility of the type in a battle.

The standard allotment of *Wespe*, *Hummel* and PzBeobWg III or IV, as it was defined during the formation of the *Panzerartillerie* in 1943, was to be fundamentally changed.

Since the *Wespe* was out of production, the number of *leichte Panzerhaubitze* (lePzHaub) was reduced in the majority of German armoured units. A total of 14 Panzer divisions were now authorized to have 12 *Hummel* and only six *Wespe*. However, only those units in *Heeresgruppe Mitte* (army group centre) were so equipped.

It is not known whether the increase in production of the *Hummel* was initiated due to problems with lePzHaub production, or on orders from Guderian who was known to want only 15cm sFH 18-armed self-propelled guns to be issued to the artillery regiments in Panzer divisions.

The authorized number to equip the seven Waffen SS divisions was not affected. By October, these divisions were in a desperate state, having lost almost all of their *Panzerartillerie*; with the exception of Wiking and Totenkopf. The number of PzBeobWg III or IV issued was drastically decreased due to

A PzKpfw IV, possibly a command tank, carries an unusual tactical mark on the track guard; a symbol used by an unknown PzArtAbt. Although a standard PzKpfw IV Ausf J cupola is fitted, it is highly possible that it was in use as an observation tank. To assist with confirmation, the officer is wearing a grey tank uniform rather than the standard *Panzerwaffe* black. Interestingly, the PzKpfw IV has been fitted with *Ostketten* (east tracks) to improve traction over thick mud, frozen road surfaces or snow.

inadequate production; instead of nine per PzArtRgt, only four were authorized. Of the 160 PzBeobWg delivered, 99 were missing, with a further 20 under repair in the workshops, leaving only 41 combat ready.

The self-propelled artillery battalions in HArtRgt at army troop level were cut back to an authorized number of 14 *Hummel* instead of 18.

In December 1944, the GenArt compiled a further list explaining the equipment situation in the *Panzerartillerie* as of 3 December. Again the shortage of *Wespe* is evident, production continued without any thought being given to losses. This was especially felt on the Western Front where the *Wespe* was desperately missed. It is interesting to note that on the Eastern Front the lack of the type was be compensated for by a number of surplus-to-requirements *Hummel*.

Late Developments

Realizing the combat advantages of the self-propelled gun in modern warfare, the *Waffenamt* and associated offices responsible for most types of armaments began planning the development of more sophisticated self-propelled guns, but

The driver (wearing headphones) and radio operator in their respective hatches on a *Hummel*; the intercom system was easily damaged, which caused some units to install a series of coloured lamps or a speaking tube to send orders to the driver. Note the thick glass blocks fitted in the driver's vision device.

due to the desperate state of German industry and the resultant production problems many would never get beyond being paper projects.

Firstly, all work to improve the guns for the divisional artillery was cancelled, including development work that had been initiated in the late 1930s. In 1943, it was accepted that the leFH and sFH-armed self-propelled guns lacked range, were too heavy and difficult to operate on the battlefield. But military planners thought their general performance was sufficient, and that no further development work was required. Thus regarding the weaponry, the proven 10.5cm leFh 18 and the 15cm sFH 18 remained in front-line service. There was an ambitious plan to use components of the new PzKpfw V Panther tank, but only wooden mock-ups were produced.

On 12 October 1944, the GenArt reported after a meeting with the *Panzerkommission*:

At the meeting on 4 October, the question as to whether to terminate production of the PzKpfw III, the PzKpfw IV and the GW III/IV was discussed. This decision would impose rigid restrictions on the artillery, since these chassis are used for the *Sturmgeschütz*, also for the *Panzerbeobachtungswagen* and for the *schwere Panzerhaubitze*. For the future advancement of the *Panzerartillerie* will result in the following:

Elements of PzArtRgt 102 in the field: In autumn 1943, 9.PzDiv had a PzKpfw II light tank surplus to requirements; subsequently it was attached to the self-propelled gun battalion for use as a PzBeobWg. The vehicle was equipped with a Fu 8 radio, and fitted with a frame-type aerial salvaged from a PzBefWg III.

1) Assault artillery

Importantly the new *Sturmgeschütz* must use the chassis 38(t) [le PzJg 38(t) *Hetzer* (Baiter)]. The development of a *Sturmhaubitze* based on the 38(t) must be accelerated. A conversion to le PzJg 38(t) will result in following:

a) Weaker amour protection.

b) Any improvement of armament and armour protection will not be possible.

c) Improvement of the penetration power of the gun will possibly rely on improved ammunition.

d) The interior space is very cramped.

e) To balance the weaker combat value [compared to the StuG] the assault artillery must be issued with *Jagdpanther* (six for each brigade).

2) Ammunition carrier

For the assault artillery an ammunition carrier base on the 38(t) has to be developed.

3) *Panzerbeobachtungswagen*

Introduction of the PzBeobWg Panther with the narrow turret is vitally important.

4) *Panzerhaubitze*

According to weapons and equipment department 6, production of le and sPzHaub will continue at 100 units per month. This output is sufficient, but only if the production of spare parts increases.

5) Recovery vehicles

For le StuG, PzBeobWg and PzHaub production of the heavy ZgKw [SdKfz 8] must be increased.

A *Hummel* is manoeuvred over semi-frozen terrain during the spring thaw on the Eastern Front. The vehicle carries four spare road wheels; two mounted on each side of the superstructure. The vehicle is fitted with Bosch headlamps and a PzKpfw IV Ausf D-type idler wheel indicating that it was produced in May 1943.

The above note shows that the GenArt was generally willing to support the plans of the OrgAbt, and that the replacement of the proven *Sturmgeschütz* III (and with reservations StuG IV) by the *leichter Panzerjäger* 38(t) *Hetzer* is as acceptable. But his acceptance was conditional on six *Jagdpanther* being issued to each brigade to give the *Sturmartillerie* the firepower he had long desired.

Quite surprisingly, there is no mention of a new *Panzerhaubitze*, possibly because the decision to continue production of the *Hummel* had already been made.

From a memorandum dated 25 October 1944:

Termination of PzKpfw III and IV production

1) Production of *Sturmgeschütz* Pz IV *lang* [Panzer IV/70 (V)], on the PzKpfw III/IV chassis will be continued until autumn 1945. This is due to problems with the conversion and the production of necessary spare parts.
2) A continuation of production of le and sPzHaub using this chassis is not intended after completion of the current order. However, it is possible that this could be postponed.
3) The *Sturmgeschütz* 38(t) (500 in service) has proved to be outstanding.
4) A *Sturmhaubitze* on 38(t) is technically feasible.

The *Hummel* Gw III/IV used many components from the PzKpfW III also the PzKpfw IV. The reason for this is unknown, but it was possibly done so as not to affect the production of PzKpfw IV tank. This particular vehicle is fitted with an early type of PzKpfw III final-drive sprocket.

A Hummel in a camouflaged position on the edge of woodland: Two spare road wheels, usually carried on the front of the superstructure, have been placed on the the radio operator´s hatch. The tactical marking for a self-propelled artillery battery is stencilled on the front of the track guard and also adjacent to the air vent.

Disribution of *Panzerartillerie* as of 3 December 1944

Army Group (Units not specified)	*leichte Panzerhaubitze*			*schwere Panzerhaubitze*		
	Target	Actual	Discrepancy	Target	Actual	Discrepancy
Eastern Front:						
Herresgruppe Süd Seven PzDiv and PzGrenDiv including two SS-PzDiv	60	12	+48	30	49	+19
Heeresgruppe 'A' Six PzDiv and PzGrenDiv	48	40	+8	24	37	+13
Heeresgruppe Mitte Ten PzDiv and PzGrenDiv including two SS-PzDiv	108	73	+35	54	55	+1
Heeresgruppe Nord Four PzDiv including one SS-PzDiv	36	29	+7	18	11	+7
Obskommando West: 14 PzDiv and PzGrenDiv including five SS-PzDiv and SS-PzGrenDiv	120	21	+99	60	24	-36
Obskommando Südwest: Four PzDiv and PzGrenDiv including one SS-PzGrenDiv	12	17	+5	6	0	-6
Total	Total			Total		
45 PzDiv and PzGrenDiv Seven SS-PzDiv and SS-PzGrenDiv	384	192	+192	192	176	+16

5) A StuK and StuH recoilless gun on a 38(t) chassis is a possibility.

6) The 38(t) is to be fitted with 220hp Tatra diesel engine.

7) *Waffenträger*: to simplify the production of a weapon carrier the type must use components from the current 38(t). All-round fire is vital and 10mm armour is to be used to reduce weight, which including weapon will be approximately 15t.

8) OrgAbt claims *Einheitslösung Waffenträger* (universal weapon carrier) for leFH, sFH and for 8.8cm guns.

9) Features:

　a) All-round fire

　b) All-round armour protection

　c) Dismountable gun

　Gun carriage that can be towed. When packed with ammunition containers the carriage can be utilized as the ammunition carrier.

10) *Hummel*

At present no deliveries are being made due to a shortage of gearboxes and engines. Depending on enemy air raids, supply can soon be resumed.

sFh auf Panther

The development of the Panther chassis to mount a sFH would be the simplest solution. If the option to dismount the gun is removed, a substantial saving can be achieved. In this case two gun carriages could be towed.

le PzHaub Alkett

The proposed le PzHaub Alkett on *Einheits-Fahrgestell* Gw III/IV is unlikely to be realized.

As noted in *Waffenmerkblatt* (weapons pamphlet) No.10, the 15cm sFH 18 mounted on the *Hummel* had an effective range of 11,200m, using a No.7 charge. For maximum range (13,250m), a No.8 charge was required, but this could only be used if a muzzle brake was fitted. The prototype was fitted with a muzzle brake, but for an unknown reason it was not used on production vehicles; perhaps military planners considered 11,200m to be sufficient.

A *Hummel* from 1.SS-PzDiv Leibstandarte Adolf Hitler carries the name 'Alfred Hansel', possibly after a comrade who had died in combat. The vehicle is parked under the cover of trees as the crew carries out routine maintenance and cleaning.

Consideration is being given to the possibility of mounting a leFH on the chassis of the *Hummel*. In this way more leFH could be issued to the *Panzerartillerie*.

The further development is best described in these extracts from a memorandum, dated 26 December 1944, from General Thomale of *Inspektion* 4 (artillery) noting the concerns of his office:

Fundamental debate regarding artillery elements in the *Panzerprogramm* 45

4.) *Schwere Panzerhaubitze*
Because of the serious delays in Panther production, Thomale requests that the targets for future developments are dropped for the time being:
· Dismounting the sFH from the carrier
· 360° all-round fire
· Instead it shall be examined as to whether it is technically possible to simply mount

the sFH on a *Waffenträger* using components of the 38(t). This carrier will use the Tatra diesel engine.

However, the GenArt insists that the type must have all-round fire, otherwise the effectiveness of the artillery in a Panzer division will be severely reduced. A final decision will have to be deferred.

The *Waffenträger* concept, developed in parallel with the *Panzerhaubitze*, was a series of different guns mounted on standardized tracked chassis, and was examined by a number of companies including Rheinmetall-Borsig and also Krupp-Steyr. These weapon carriers were to be a simple tracked vehicle with the engine and transmission mounted in the front part of the chassis, and a pedestal-type mounting for the gun (to allow a 360° traverse) positioned on the rear. Because of the requirement to dismount the gun a conventional turret was not used, and instead it would be fitted with a large box-like gun shield.

Although a tempting and a future-looking project, it would not be feasible to mass produce the *Waffenträger*.

Artillerie-Lehr-Regiment (ALR – artillery training regiment) at Jüterbog had a number of vehicles for training purposes. The *Hummel* is an early production vehicle and carries the German-style 'L' for Lehr; the numeral indicates gun battery No.9.

The five-man crew of a *Hummel* preparing the gun to fire on the training grounds of the Artillerie Lehr-Regiment, Jüterbog. Note the early type exhaust muffler; this was removed from later vehicles due to the ingress of dangerous exhaust gases.

5.) Production proportion between light and heavy *Panzerhaubitze*

Thomale repeated his fundamental demand to equip the entire *Panzerartillerie* with only the *Hummel*. After a thorough briefing on the ammunition situation and current production capacity, Thomale agreed to expand production of the *leichte Panzerhaubitze*, at a ratio of three *leichte* to one *schwere Panzerhaubitze* for the time being. When (if) the situation with the supply ammunition changes, production will then be immediately switched to the *schwere Panzerhaubitze*.

The *Waffenträger* (weapon carrier) project was one of the many ideas to introduce economical and effective multi-purpose self-propelled guns for the artillery and the *Panzerjäger*. Rheinmetall-Borsig designed a vehicle which utilized components from the PzKpfw 38(t) and at first was fitted with the 8.8cm PaK 43, but the type did not progress beyond the prototype stage.

In April 1944, the GenArt announced that production of the *Wespe* had ended and that present demand for self-propelled guns would be met by an increase in production of *schwere Panzerhaubitze Hummel*. However a short time later, there was a considerable slump in the production of the *Hummel*: in June only four were completed and none in July. In August 1944, production had increased to 50 units, the same rate as in February and not sufficient to meet requirements.

Ersatz Wespe

While production of the *Wespe* was ceased no direct replacement had been found. At around this date it was clear that production of the 10.5cm

Since no successor for the *Wespe* was in sight, it was decided to use the Gw III/IV to mount a 10.5cm leFH 18/40. The type was occasionally known as an '*Ersatz Wespe*' (replacement *Wespe*), but only a small number were built by end of the war.

Heuschrecke, to be manufactured by Krupp and Alkett, would not take place.

Instead it was decided to mount a 10.5cm leFH 18 on the *Hummel* chassis, which was to remain in production, as a simple way to provide the artillery with leFH self-propelled guns. The chassis was used virtually unchanged, but the requirement for the gun to be dismountable was dropped.

Production was to start almost immediately of the type which was occasionally referred to as an *Ersatz-Wespe* (substitute *Wespe*). On 11 December 1944, GenArt reported that documentation for the design had been signed and also a production order for 250 units for delivery in June 1945. Production was scheduled to commence in February 1945 at a rate of 80 units per month.

But on 10 February 1945 the OKH announced:

> Due to the drop in leFH production, delivery of the 250 *le Panzerhaubitze auf Fahrgestell Hummel* is no longer anticipated. Instead of the 80 lePzHaub scheduled for February only ten will be completed, followed by another 20 in March. To compensate, production of *Panzerhaubitzen* will proceed as follows:
> In parallel with the highest possible output of le PzHaub, some 50 sPzHaub (*Hummel* with 15cm sFH 18) will be produced. The available 80 sFH guns from the *Hummel* production

will be mounted on *Beutelafetten* (captured gun mounts). Production of le PzHaub (leFH on a *Hummel* chassis) will be fixed at 200 and not 250 units.

Waffenamt suggests the use of the 15.2cm sFH 433(r) and 15.2cm KH 433(r), due to its much lower weight.

It is thought that a total of 11 *Ersatz Wespe* had been produced by the end of the year.

10.5cm leFH 18 auf le ZgKw 3t

At the same time as production of the *Wespe* ended, Alkett demonstrated some self-propelled guns to the GenArt at Hillersleben firing range. Two were versions of the *Heuschrecke*, which had already been accepted for limited production, the other an SdKfz 11 half-track vehicle which had been modified to mount a leFH. A similar type, a partly armoured ZgKw 3t (SdKfz 11) mounting a 2cm FlaK 38, had been ordered into production in late 1943. Also presented was similar vehicle mounting an 8.8cm PaK 43.

The crew has carefully concealed this early production *Hummel* in bushes in the Russian countryside. The large crates placed on the vehicle contain cartridges for the 15cm sFH 18 heavy field howitzer. Near the edge of the front plate are the two armoured domes covering the cooling air inlets for the susceptible steering brakes.

Officers from 2.SS-PzDiv
Das Reich converse behind
the cover of a PzBeobWg III;
a PzKpfw IV from the
Panzer regiment is in the
background. The vehicle is
fitted with a *Sterantenne*
(star antenna) which was
far less conspicuous than
the previous frame-type
aerial.

It is worth noting that the GenArt supported immediate production of the leFH on a half-track chassis and further trials confirmed that it was a viable project. Sadly no further details are known.

On 14 May, the GenArt made his report on current ordnance projects and suggested that many of a series of projects for the artillery should be cancelled. Among those to be continued was the 10.5cm leFH 18 *auf* ZgKw 3t (SdKfz 11).

On 29 September 1944, GenArt ordered two officers (General Scheffler and Major Wettig) to visit *Artillerieschule* II to examine the leFH auf ZgKw 3t and reported:

> The training officer emphasized that he assumed that the leFH will be fired from the 3-ton half-track vehicle; this Scheffler denied. In general the gun would be fired from its ground mounting to save the vehicle from unnecessary damage. The gun would only be fired when on the vehicle in a special situation, for instance during combat in towns or around wooded areas. For the battery of six guns only two hoists would be available, and this was regarded as being sufficient.

In late 1944, trials were carried out to mount the 10.5cm leFH 18 on the chassis of a le ZgKw 3t (SdKfz 11) half-track vehicle. Although the gun could provide all-round fire, the weight of the weapon severely overloaded the vehicle. After being tested in a stone quarry, the six vehicles built were deployed against Allied forces in the fighting around Hannover.

Late production *Munitionspanzer* (ammunition carrier) had a wider more spacious compartment for the driver and also the radio operator. The embrasure for the gun was simply plated over.

Assembly of the type appeared straightforward by using components from production of the SdKfz 251. An open-topped superstructure was to be used and the gun was fitted on a pedestal-type mounting positioned in the centre of the chassis, directly behind the driver. Two of the six vehicles built had brackets fitted for the gun hoists.

On 11 December 1944, GenArt reported that production of the type at the Hanomag facility was delayed due to heavy bombing raids. A short time later, the company did manage to complete six vehicles which were then taken to a quarry near Hannover for firing trials. In January 1945, the six vehicles were used to establish a trial battery and issued to ArtRgt 33 with 15.PzGrenDiv.

The guns were used in combat against US and British troops as they advanced towards Germany. A number of veterans who served on the guns have stated the battery suffered no losses and that their vehicles were handed over to the Allied forces after the armistice.

Panzerartillerie – An Appraisal

While the value of the tank had been recognized long before World War II, many nations had differing views on how to deploy the vehicle known as the 'Queen of the Battlefield'.

Great Britain and France decided that the new weapon would be used as cavalry in support the infantry, but history shows that Germany chose a different course. Their superior and highly mobile tank force would set the pace in the conflict to come.

In an attack, a Panzer division would have fully motorized rifle regiments to follow and support the tanks.

The artillery (conventional towed infantry and divisional artillery), also known as the 'Queen of the Battlefield', would deliver a bombardment to launch an attack, but as the subsequent advance began would not be able to keep pace with speed of the tanks.

The decision by military planners to develop self-propelled artillery was obvious, but the omnipresent shortage of raw materials, lack of industrial capacity and the shortage of finance caused many delays. It is quite understandable that the first self-propelled guns were merely an interim solution.

Some two years after Germany invaded France, the first advanced infantry self-propelled guns would be issued to front-line units on a large scale. In 1943, new types mounting heavier guns began to enter service.

By 1944, self-propelled artillery units had become an integral part of all Panzer and *Panzergrenadier* divisions. Many after-action reports confirm the value of the type.

Both the *Wespe* and *Hummel* were very mobile and could be positioned (or withdrawn) much faster than units equipped with half-tracked tractors – whatever the terrain.

The susceptibility of the final-drive units and running gear on the *Wespe* and *Hummel*, and also the PzBeobWg III would constantly affect operational readiness in mud and snow, and especially in the mountains of Italy.

Germany was the first nation in World War II to introduce self-propelled artillery on a large scale to front-line units. But it happened late and utilized the hull and running gear of obsolete types such as the PzKpfw II, PzKpfw III and early versions of the PzKpfw IV. More modern and sophisticated types were being developed, but the armaments industry was unable to deliver.

It is somewhat ironic that this very effective offensive weapon entered service at a time when German units were retreating on all fronts. In final days of the war, any offensive operation, even on a small scale, became the absolute exception.

Self-Propelled Artillery Distribution as of 1 October 1944 (Actual Strengths)

Unit/Army Group	Modified organization	leichte Panzerhaubitze			
		Target	Combat ready	Under repair	Discrepancy
Heeresgruppe Süd					
24.PzDiv	Yes	6	2	0	-4
13.PzDiv	Yes	6	2	0	-4
1.PzDiv	Yes	0	0	0	0
23.PzDiv		12	10	2	0
PzGrenDiv 'FHH'	Yes	6	0	0	-6
Heeresgruppe 'A'					
HArtAbt 101	Yes	0	0	0	0
8.PzDiv	Yes	6	3	6	+3
HArtAbt 1042		12	8	2	-2
16.PzDiv		12	12	1	+1
17.PzDiv		12	10	3	+1
II./ArtRgt 71	Yes	0	0	0	0
Heeresgruppe Mitte					
25.PzDiv		12	6	0	-6
19.PzDiv	Yes	6	5	1	0
II./ArtRgt 63	Yes	0	0	0	0
6.PzDiv	Yes	6	5	1	0
3.PzDiv		12	10	1	-1
I./HArtBrig 88	Yes	6	5	2	+1
5.PzDiv		12	17	0	+5
FS PzDiv 'HG'		12	12	6	+6
PzGrenDiv 'GD'	Yes	6	4	2	0
7.PzDiv		12	8	4	0
HArtAbt 845	Yes	0	0	0	0
Heeresgruppe Nord					
14.PzDiv		12	8	1	-3
12.PzDiv		12	10	1	-1
4.PzDiv		12	10	1	-1
HArtAbt 536	Yes	0	0	0	0
(continued overleaf)					

schwere Panzerhaubitze				PzBeobWg III/IV			
Target	Combat ready	Under repair	Discrepancy	Target	Combat ready	Under repair	Discrepancy
12	7	3	-2	4	3	0	-1
12	1	0	-11	4	0	0	-4
18	0	0	-18	4	2	1	-1
6	3	1	-3	4	1	0	-3
12	0	0	-12	4	0	0	-4
14	10	2	-2	0	0	0	0
12	11	2	+1	4	0	4	0
6	4	0	+2	0	0	0	0
6	6	1	+1	4	1	0	-3
6	6	1	+1	4	1	0	-3
14	7	4	-3	0	0	0	0
6	5	1	0	4	4	1	1
12	10	2	0	4	1	1	-2
14	11	1	-2	0	0	0	0
12	11	2	+1	4	2	0	-2
6	5	1	0	4	0	0	-4
12	8	4	0	4	0	0	-4
6	8	0	+2	4	0	0	-4
6	5	1	0	4	2	1	-1
12	11	0	-1	4	1	0	-3
6	10	1	+5	4	1	0	-3
14	11	2	-1	0	0	0	0
6	2	1	-3	4	2	1	-1
6	4	0	-2	4	1	2	-1
6	3	0	-3	4	4	1	+1
14	10	4	0	0	0	0	0

Unit/Army Group	Modified organization	leichte Panzerhaubitze			
		Target	Combat ready	Under repair	Discrepancy
Dänemark					
233.Res PzDiv			2		
Oberkommando West					
9.PzDiv	Yes	6	0	1	-5
3.PzGrenDiv	Yes	18	0	0	-18
116.PzDiv	Yes	6	2	0	-4
2.PzDiv		12	0	1	-11
11.PzDiv	Yes	6	4	4	+2
21.PzDiv	Yes	6	0	0	-6
PzLehrDiv	Yes	6	0	0	-6
Heeresgruppe 'C'					
90.PzGrenDiv	Yes	18	6	2	-10
26.PzDiv		12	5	0	0
29.PzGrenDiv	Yes	18	0	0	-18
BdE (replacment army)					
1.PzDiv	Yes	0	0	0	0
20.PzDiv	Yes	12	0	0	-12
Führer GrenBrig	Yes	0	0	0	0
SS Panzer Divisions					
1.LAH		12	0	0	-12
2.Das Reich		12	0	0	-12
3.Totenkopf		12	8	0	-4
5.Wiking		12	15	1	+4
9.Hohenstaufen		12	0	0	-12
10.Frundsberg		12	0	0	-12
12.Hitlerjugend		12	0	0	-12
Totals		396	189	43	+164

schwere Panzerhaubitze			
Target	Combat ready	Under repair	Discrepancy
	2		
12	3	2	-7
0	0	0	0
12	5	4	-3
6	0	0	+6
12	2	2	-8
12	0	0	-12
12	0	0	-12
0	0	0	0
6	1	0	-5
0	0	0	0
18	0	0	0
6	0	0	-6
18	0	0	-18
6	0	0	-6
6	0	0	-6
6	9	1	+4
6	7	1	+2
6	0	0	-6
6	0	0	-6
6	0	0	-6
412	198	44	170

PzBeobWg III/IV			
Target	Combat ready	Under repair	Discrepancy
	5		
4	0	0	-4
4	2	0	-2
4	0	0	-4
4	0	0	-4
4	2	4	+2
4	1	1	-2
4	0	0	-4
4	1	0	-3
4	1	1	-2
4	0	1	-3
4	0	0	0
4	0	0	-4
4	0	0	-4
4	0	0	-4
4	3	1	0
4	0	0	-4
4	0	0	-4
4	0	0	-4
4	0	0	-4
4	0	0	-4
160	41	20	+99

INDEX

ACKNOWLEDGEMENTS

Much of the information in this book has been researched from a number of public archives; primarily the Bundesarchiv/Militärarchiv, Freiburg, Germany, and the National Archives and Records Administrations (NARA), Washington, USA. A new source is the internet-based 'Project for Digitizing German Documents in the Archives of the Russian Federation', where I discovered a number of interesting documents which, after careful evaluation, have been used to confirm historical detail.

Further research was completed by referring to a very small number of post-war printed publications: an excellent reference source is the *Panzer Tracts* series.

I would like to express heartfelt thanks to the following individuals who have provided not only help and advice, but also access to their own collections:

Karlheinz Münch, Peter Kocsis, Henry Hoppe and Holger Erdmann

As many times before; sincere thanks to my editor, Jasper Spencer-Smith, an indomitable and ever-patient gentleman.

Unless otherwise indicated, all the images in this book are from the Thomas Anderson Collection.

Bibliography

Panzertruppen Volume 1 and Volume 2; Tom Jentz: Schiffer, Atglen, PA, USA
Panzer Tracts, several volumes: Panzer Tracts, Boyds, MD, USA
Nuts & Bolts, several editions: Canfora Publishing, Stockholm, Sweden
Waffen Revue, several editions: Journal Verlag Schwend GmbH, Germany